Tax Guide 300

ORGANIZING YOUR ESTATE

by

Holmes F. Crouch
Tax Specialist

Published by

Allyear Tax Guides
20484 Glen Brae Drive
Saratoga, CA 95070

ISBN-13: 9780944817810
ISBN-10: 0944817815

LCCN 2006930825

Printed in U.S.A.

Series 300
Retirees & Estates

Tax Guide 303

ORGANIZING YOUR ESTATE

For other titles in print, see page 224.

The author: **Holmes F. Crouch**
For more about the author, see page 221.

PREFACE

If you are a knowledge-seeking **taxpayer** looking for information, this book can be helpful to you. It is designed to be read — from cover to cover — in less than eight hours. Or, it can be "skim-read" in about 30 minutes.

Either way, you are treated to **tax knowledge** . . . *beyond the ordinary*. The "beyond" is that which cannot be found in IRS publications, FedWorld on-line services, tax software programs, Internet chatrooms, or E-mail bulletins.

Taxpayers have different levels of interest in a selected subject. For this reason, this book starts with introductory fundamentals and progresses onward. You can verify the progression by chapter and section in the table of contents. In the text, "applicable law" is quoted in pertinent part. Key phrases and key tax forms are emphasized. Real-life examples are given . . . in down-to-earth style.

This book has 12 chapters. This number provides depth without cross-subject rambling. Each chapter starts with a head summary of meaningful information.

To aid in your skim-reading, informative diagrams and tables are placed strategically throughout the text. By leafing through page by page, reading the summaries and section headings, and glancing at the diagrams and tables, you can get a good handle on the matters covered.

Effort has been made to update and incorporate all of the latest tax law changes that are *significant* to the title subject. However, "beyond the ordinary" does not encompass every conceivable variant of fact and law that might give rise to protracted dispute and litigation. Consequently, if a particular statement or paragraph is crucial to your own specific case, you are urged to seek professional counseling. Otherwise, the information presented is general and is designed for a broad range of reader interests.

The Author

INTRODUCTION

IRS Form 706: Ever heard of it? Ever seen it? Ever held it? Ever filled one out? Probably not.

Form 706 is a *death* tax return. Its short title is: ***U.S. Estate Tax Return***. Its full title is: ***U.S. Estate (and Generation-Skipping Transfer) Tax Return***. The form itself is 40 pages long. Ordinarily, it is prepared by your executor after your death. Yet it is one of those rare tax forms that you can initiate on your own before death, to organize the preparation for your own demise.

In year 2000, Form 706 was required for gross estates exceeding $600,000 at time of death. In 2001, Congress decided to repeal the estate tax in its entirety. It did this by enacting Public Law 107-16: ***Economic Growth and Tax Relief Reconciliation Act***. To prepare for repeal, Congress increased the filing threshold for Form 706 to $675,000 in 2001; to $1,000,000 in 2002 and 2003; to $1,500,000 in 2004 and 2005; to $2,000,000 in 2006, 2007, and 2008; and to $3,500,000 in 2009. Beginning in 2010, new carryover basis rules will replace the current step-up to fair market value rules for property acquired from a decedent.

To implement this major change in tax policy, Congress also enacted a new **Section 1022** of the Internal Revenue Code. Its subsection (a) reads in principal part as—

(1)   *Property acquired from a decedent dying after December 31, 2009, shall be treated . . . as **transferred by gift**, and*

(2)   *the [tax] basis of the person acquiring [such] property . . .* ***shall be the lesser of—***

    (A)   *the adjusted basis of the decedent, or*

    (B   *the fair market value of the property at the date of the decedent's death.*

The net effect of this new tax code section is the replacement of a 45% death tax with a 15% capital gains tax. This is perhaps the most dramatic tax reduction effort ever. We'll explain herein the ramifications of how this all takes place.

In the meantime, do not draw any false inferences from repeal of the estate tax. Not only will Form 706 continue to be required, but Form 709: *U.S. Gift Tax Return*, will take on new importance for *Organizing Your Estate*. Commencing in 2006, Form 709 enables you to give up to $12,000 *per year*, **per donee** to your heirs, with no tax consequences to you . . . nor to them! Further, up through 2010, there is no limit to the number of donees, nor to the number of years you can make such gifts, called: *annual exclusions*. You do not want to go to your grave without taking advantage of these annual gift exclusions.

Even if your gross estate does not exceed the threshold filing amounts cited previously, Form 706 is a very useful planning device. It categorizes your marketable assets into nine groupings, and reminds you of the proper estate accounting for debts, expenses, and co-ownerships. The nine asset schedules comprising Form 706 are—

A — Real Estate
B — Stocks and Bonds
C — Mortgages, Notes, and Cash
D — Insurance on Decedent's Life
E — Jointly Owned Property
F — Other Miscellaneous Property
G — Transfers During Decedent's life
H — Powers of Appointment
I — Annuities

Do you have any idea at all what these schedules require of you? Wouldn't you like to know before your demise? If so, you have a FORM 706 TASK to perform.

Once you have completed your active occupational years, your "Form 706 Task" takes on special meaning. After filling out the 706, even in the most preliminary way, you'll become that RARE PERSON who truly understands what his (or her) final tax accounting is all about. Such understanding will definitely help you simplify and expedite the transfer of assets to your heirs.

CONTENTS

1

PRECAUTIONS WITH ATTORNEYS

When A Person Dies, An ESTATE Is Created By Operation Of Law. If Its GROSS VALUE Exceeds Certain Exemption Amounts, IRS Form 706 Is Required. Said Return Can Be Prepared By An Attorney, An Accountant, Or An "Enrolled Agent" (Licensed By the IRS). There's An Ongoing Tug-Of-War As To Who Can Claim Priority For Form 706 Preparation. Attorneys Get A 2% COMMISSION For Doing So; Accountants May Get A 1% Commission; Whereas Enrolled Agents Get An Hourly Fee, Unrelated To the Value Of The Decedent's Gross Estate. We Cite True Life Examples Of How The Tug-Of-War Plays Out With Attorneys.

On our front cover, we used the expression: *While thinkingly alive.* We did this intentionally. Our emphasis is on while **thinkingly alive**; not just being alive. This is the precondition for organizing your estate. You need to be aware of what you are doing, and why. You need to know what property you have, what debts you have, and which heirs are deserving of the fruits of your life-long labor. For start-thinking purposes, you need to know — right now — the dollar value of your gross estate.

In testamentary parlance — for the preparation of wills and trusts — the term "thinkingly alive" means having a sound and responsible mind. It also means having adequate physical senses (eyesight, hearing, speaking, and ambulation) and being "in control" (so to speak) when directing your estate to others.

What happens so often is that otherwise thinking persons put off prescribing their gratuitous intentions until it is far too late. Being "too late" means that your mental faculties are starting to lose their sharp edge; your energy level is waning to the point where your list of things "to do" becomes increasingly burdensome . . . and rarely ever completed. When seeing this of you, family members, friends, and advisors start prodding and persuading you to let some prestigious attorney or legal firm do all your thinking for you. "Put it all in a trust," they urge, "and everything will be taken care of." Really? If you believe this, you also probably believe in fairy tales.

Yes, of course, there are bona fide situations where estate planning attorneys are needed. But they are not needed for the type of thinking herein that you can do on your own. Nor are they needed for tasks that nonattorneys can do.

Attorneys, by training, temperament, and guile are problem creators; they are not problem solvers. They are task procrastinators; they are not task doers. They can mess up more things than they can clear up. They are intimidating and obfuscating. Since it is we who have observed these characteristics, we have a duty to cite some bad examples of what we mean. We all can learn from bad examples. There are simply more of them than those which are good.

Janitor With Two Daughters

Our first case involves a high-school graduate janitor with a wife and two adult daughters. The younger daughter had two minor children of her own, and had gone through divorce. Her ex-husband was unemployed and thus unable to pay alimony and child support. This left the younger daughter financially destitute, though she did have a low-paying job. She was highly distressed.

The father wanted to comfort his daughter by helping her acquire ownership in a condominium home. He asked his tax preparer if there were any tax benefits that could be derived by doing so. The preparer showed him Section 280A(d)(3)(C) of the Internal Revenue Code. That section is titled: *Shared Equity Financial Agreement; Rental to Family Member for Use as Principal Residence*. After the preparer read the law and its regulations to the father, the father decided to go ahead. He was thereupon urged to have an attorney draw up the agreement, and title the condo in such a way that the daughter became the 60% owner and her parents became the 40% owner. This arrangement worked quite well for about 10 years. Disabled by a serious foot injury, the father died in early 2006.

At a family meeting discussing estate matters, the mother agreed that the sharing arrangement should be terminated and that the condo be quit-claim deeded 100% to the occupying daughter. The services of an attorney were obtained.

A Pandora's box of legal options was opened up. The attorney urged that an irrevocable trust be created and that the mother's home, daughter's condo, and father's death benefits and bank accounts be deeded to it. After the mother died and after the youngest grandchild reached age 25, all estate assets would be distributed equally to both daughters. The attorney wanted a $5,000 retainer to do the initial paperwork involved.

The attorney's proposal overwhelmed and traumatized the mother. She was 80 years old at the time. The younger daughter was terrified. The attorney had led her to believe that it was illegal for the mother to quit-claim her 40% share to her daughter. When questioned on this by the older daughter, the attorney "snowed" her with details of IRS Form 706: *U.S. Estate Tax Return*, and that nothing could be done until all death taxes had been determined and paid. This infuriated the older daughter. She told her mother **not** to pay the $5,000 retainer fee, and to seek another attorney elsewhere.

No IRS Form 706 whatsoever was required. The gross estate was substantially less than $2,000,000. This was the exemption amount for persons dying (when the father died) in year 2006. (Recall the list of death tax exemption amounts on page v of our Introduction.) The attorney knew this. He was casting for control of the estate via his cobweb of trust theatrics: never-ending contingencies and options.

The "Scenario" of a Trust

We need to amplify our last statement above. When you go to any estate attorney to discuss family succession matters, inevitably the virtues of a trust will be gushed at you. A trust is pushed as a priority over wills, over gifts, over joint tenancies, over affidavits, and over powers of attorney for business and health decisions. If you question or express uncertainty over the need for a trust at that moment, the horrors of probate proceedings, estate tax filings, and wealth squandering will pour forth at you. You get a little queasy. Your mind becomes confused, and fear and fright overcome you. You get no simple, one-step-at-a-time guidance to ponder and pursue. It seems like all estate attorneys prefer to cobweb you rather than inform you. Once they get you into their trust clutches, you lose control over your estate affairs.

In all fairness, we point out that trusts do have some advantages. We can think of three practical benefits. One, a trust (before death) **may** avoid probate. It will avoid probate. . . IF . . . each class of property holdings (real estate, securities, bank accounts, and tangible items) is titled in the name of the trust before your demise. Otherwise, if there is any successor dispute over any item of property, probate proceedings are required. When this happens attorney fees go wild.

There is a second advantage to a trust. That is, the trustor (property owner) can schedule incremental and successive distributions of property over long periods of time. In contrast, distributions (bequests) via a will are one-time only. Yet, one-time distributions have advantages of their own, via cash and liquidity pools within your estate. We'll develop these matters in later chapters. In the meantime, we must tell you that incremental distributions via trust create annual income tax filings (via IRS Form 1041). Often, there is confusion among the trustee(s) and beneficiaries as to when the extended trust shall terminate.

The third advantage is wealth preservation and the creation of wealth dynasties. If a trustor's gross estate exceeds, say, $100,000,000 (100 million), there is a natural desire to want to preserve this wealth on down through generational lines. This is the modus operandi of generation-skipping trusts. Some transfer tax savings accrue . . . at the expense of extreme complexity. Wealth preservation trusts are a fee bonanza for trust departments of banks and for those attorneys who supervise such trusts.

Has your estate attorney explained these and other related matters to you? Or, are you left bewildered and confused?

Trust Format Simplified

Before you succumb to trust euphoria, some introductory commentary on trust format could be instructive. Most family trusts are created by a husband and wife designated as Trustors. Until both decease, they are also trustees of their own trust. Upon the latter of the two deaths, successor trustees are designated in the trust instrument. Included also is the designation of heirs and other recipients of trust property, and the portions to each. The "trust property" is identified in an Exhibit A that is attached directly to the instrument. This "instrument" titled: *Declaration of Trust*, when signed and notarized becomes a 20- to 35-page legal document. The first three pages identify the trustors, trustee, trust property, and property recipients. All other pages are boilerplate: contingencies, order of deaths, resolution of disputes, etc.

The general arrangement of a family trust is portrayed in Figure 1.1. Note that on the first death of a trustor, three subtrusts are formed. Each is designated separately as: A — The Bypass Trust, B — The Marital Trust, and C — The Survivor's Trust. Other variant names of these subtrusts may apply. The assumption is that the combined gross estates of the husband and wife trustors exceed the amount required for filing IRS Form 706.

Subtrust A (the bypass trust) is so named because it comprises that amount of property which is statutorily exempt from estate taxation at time of death. Alternatively, it may be named the Exemption Trust (for death year _____).

Subtrust B (the marital trust) is so named because it comprises that property listed on Schedule **M** (for "married"?) of Form 706. The Schedule M is titled: *Bequests, etc., to Surviving Spouse*. Items listed on this schedule are deductible against the decedent's estate, **provided** they are included in the surviving spouse's estate. Alternatively, the marital trust may be named the Marital Deduction Trust (a better description, we believe).

Subtrust C (the survivor's trust) is so named because it comprises the surviving trustor's gross estate independent of the decedent trustor's estate. This subtrust is subject to a separate estate taxation process of its own when the surviving trustor dies. At that time, there is a coalescence of the residual/distributable estates of the two trustors.

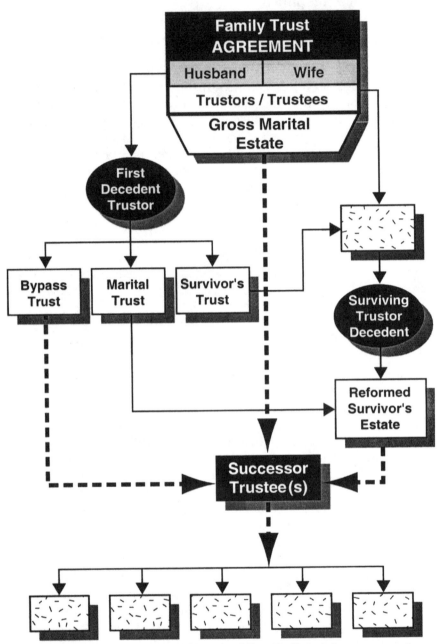

Fig. 1.1 - Diagram of Classical Family Trust Arrangement

Thereafter, a new series of subtrusts is created to respond to the distributional intentions in the trust instrument. Among the new subtrust options are: child support trusts (a separate trust for each minor child), educational trusts (for those qualifying for higher learning), special needs trusts (for the disabled and handicapped regardless of age), annuity trusts (for senior heirs), spendthrift trusts (for heirs who squander money), generation-skipping trusts, charitable remainder trusts, etc., etc.

Our point is that the ongoing subtrust options are endless. Unless restrained by trustee emphatics or dwindling trust money, attorneys will subtrust ad infinitum. Now, let us continue with our dialogue of attorney bad examples.

Deceased Pilot, Disabled Wife

An 85-year-old retired airline pilot and his 82-year-old wife were on a vacation trip by auto. They were hit by a long-haul truck and trailer. The wife was paralyzed from the hips on down, and suffered a mild stroke. Although the husband was only slightly injured externally, he died about two years later from internal injuries. A family trust had been prepared many years earlier, naming their two daughters as sole beneficiaries.

After all memorial services were over, the wife called for a meeting of her attorney, her financial advisor, her husband's tax preparer, and the couple's two adult daughters. In estate meetings like this, the attorney is front and center, and takes charge. The attorney promptly announced that she had "authority from the IRS" to issue EINs (Employer Identification Number) for each of the three subtrusts: Bypass, Marital, and Survivor's (described above). An EIN is an identification number for an entity, similar to an SSN for an individual. EINs are issued by the IRS for tax administration purposes solely.

"Authority from the IRS?" Such a statement by an attorney is baloney! Anybody can apply for an EIN when needed.

An attorney has no more "authority" to issue EINs than does a nonattorney. **Any** third party designee can prepare IRS Form SS-4: *Application for Employer Identification Number*, phone the IRS, and get an EIN assigned on the spot. A "designee" is a person designated by the executor (of a decedent's estate) or by the trustee (of an irrevocable trust) to receive tax information. The designee does not sign Form SS-4; the executor or trustee does. The executor or trustee signs: *Under penalties of perjury*, etc. See figure 1.2 for an abridged version of Form SS-4.

Form SS-4	Application For EMPLOYER IDENTIFICATION NUMBER	EIN _____

Name of entity:	Executor, trustee, "care of"
_____	_____

Name of owner, grantor, trustor:	SSN or EIN
_____	_____

TYPE OF ENTITY:
[16 options]

☐ Estate (SSN of decedent) _____
☐ Trust (SSN of grantor) _____
☐ Other (specify) _____

REASON FOR APPLYING:
[9 options]

☐ Creation of trust (specify type) _____
_____
☐ Other (specify) _____

3rd Party Designee — *Complete ONLY if you want to authorize the named individual to receive the EIN & other entity information.*

Name, address, phone, & fax numbers: _____

APPLICANT

Name & title; phone & fax: _____

/s/ *Signature*   Date:

Under penalties of perjury... I declare this application... to be true, correct, and complete.

Fig. 1.2 - Portions of IRS Form SS-4 re Estates & Trusts

As it turned out in the situation above, the attorney prepared two SS-4 forms and submitted them to the older daughter for signing as the trustee. One SS-4 was for the Bypass Trust, the other was for the Marital Trust. The attorney had entered her own name as designee for each subtrust. She also entered a pre-assigned EIN for each SS-4 that she had obtained from the IRS by phone. This enabled the attorney to charge high legal fees for clerical type tasks.

Realistically, the attorney's EIN application tasks were premature. The decedent died in January; the EINs were assigned in March: just two months later. Ordinarily, when a person dies, an **Estate** (not a trust) is created by operation of law. This requires that, when applicable, IRS Form 706: *U.S. Estate (Transfer) Tax Return* be prepared, submitted, and accepted by the IRS before the decedent's estate is settled and the trust estate is established. The IRS allows nine months for completion of Form 706, and may grant a six-month extension if requested.

Rather than a trust EIN, the attorney (as designee) should have signified an estate EIN. An EIN is not used on Form 706: it is the decedent's SSN that is used. However, an EIN is required on IRS Form 1041: *U.S. Income Tax Return for Estates and Trusts*. Note official order of wording: "Estates and Trusts," NOT "Trusts and Estates." Either way, Form 1041 is due (ordinarily) on April 15 of the year following year of death. There was plenty of time to engage in the EIN tasks.

Why the Bypass Trust Rush?

Let us continue with our true life example above. Doing so, we are compelled to ask: "Why was there such a rush to get trust EINs — especially for the Bypass Trust — so early in the death year?" You have a hint to the answer when we tell you that the marital gross estate (husband and wife) well exceeded $5,000,000 (5 million dollars).

For the year of death (2006), a decedent's estate can carve out and set aside up to $2,000,000 (2 million) as the death tax exemption amount. (Recall the year-of-death list of exemption amounts on page v of our Introduction.) This means that for a marital estate of $5 million, the decedent's Form 706 estate would be $2.5 million (or so). And, since the attorney was the trustee-approved designee, who had obtained a pre-assigned EIN, the attorney was in a position to supervise and control the management of a $2 million bypass trust. Do you get the point? Two million dollars is abundant collateral for assuring payment of all attorney fees, regardless of how long the 706 filing is dragged out.

The attorney then proceeded to direct the stock brokerage firm (the decedent was an avid investor) to earmark specific stocks, bonds, and money market accounts to the bypass trust. The attorney directed what the name of the trust should be, and that a new brokerage account be set up with the pre-assigned EIN. The attorney went so far as to designate 49 stocks (valued at $1,297,081), 2 bonds (valued at $478,393), and five money markets (valued at $224,526) as trust assets. The grand total came to $2,000,000 . . . precisely.

Being in a stock brokerage account, the $2,000,000 death tax exemption amount was liquid and available to the surviving spouse at any time. But the same amount would have been also available to the spouse *without* its being in a trust (early in the death year).

As it turned out, the motivation behind the bypass trust rush was the decedent's two daughters. Both were designated by their mother (the surviving spouse) as co-trustees for the $2,000,000 account. Both daughters were married, had modest incomes, and had children of their own. Each had read various books and newsletters on investment strategies and on the virtues of wealth preservation via trusts. They both envisioned parlaying the $2 million to $10 million or more. And they so instructed their financial advisor (stock broker) accordingly. Thus, not only was the attorney assured of her extensive fees, the stock broker (a female) was also assured of her commissions on frequent stock churnings . . . year in and year out.

Widow with Alcoholic Daughter

A husband and wife each were successful real estate agents and brokers. In their nearly 50 years of marriage, they had accumulated real estate holdings worth over $10 million (in 2006 dollars). The husband died first from natural causes. Ten years later the wife died (also from natural causes). The husband had named the couple's three children as co-trustees, and directed that Form 706 and annual Forms 1041 be prepared by the couple's long-time tax representative.

The wife directed that her estate be handled exclusively by the older daughter (later described as alcoholic). Because both spouses were well known in real estate circles in the area, an elaborate obituary notice for the wife was published in local newspapers, giving the date and place of memorial services.

At the memorial services, an attorney (entirely unknown to family members) showed up. He sauntered among the attendees and inquired as to the identity of the children. He introduced himself to each and learned that the older daughter (the middle child was a son) was the designated executor for the estate.

About 10 days later, the three children (all adults) met with the mother's tax preparer to do the father's Form 1041. They also supplied information to do their mother's Form 706. Included were professional appraisals on the mother's nearly $7 million of realty holdings. The preparer pulled from his files the 40-page Form 706 and read to them portions thereof. He further explained the nine gross estate schedules and the five deduction schedules required. He estimated that his fee would be around $10,000 to prepare the form. The older daughter wrote a check to the preparer for $2,000 and told him to get started.

Within two weeks, the tax preparer had completed the 16 checkbox general information questionnaire, all of Schedule A: **Real Estate** and the preliminary portions of other schedules. A few days later, out of the blue, the executor phoned the tax preparer to discharge him and request the $2,000 back.

The daughter said that the attorney she had met at her mother's memorial services told her: "It is illegal for a tax preparer to do IRS Form 706 because it is 'practicing law' to do so." The preparer tried to explain that he was IRS-licensed to do Form 706. She was adamant and would not listen. Obligingly, the preparer returned $1,000 to her.

When the younger daughter learned of this, she became angry and upset. She phoned the tax preparer to reveal that the older daughter was a chronic alcoholic. She also revealed that before her mother died, there were many family arguments over her sister's alcoholism. She was in a stupor most of the time, and was incapable of making sound judgments. After turning everything over to the attorney, she drank more and more.

There's a little "secret" that attorneys don't want you to know about: their commission on the decedent's gross estate. Under California's probate code (CPC), for example, an attorney can charge approximately a 2% commission for simply *signing* IRS Form 706 [CPC § 10800(a)]. On the nearly $7,000,000 widow's estate above, that would be close to $140,000 in the attorney's pocket! But, that's not all. He can charge additional compensation for his legal services and can add other fees for hiring tax persons to do all of the tax work re Form 706 and Forms 1041 [CPC § 10801(a), (b)]. The tax persons are paid a *fee* (NOT a commission) that is payable from the estate.

The express wording on Form 706 that relates to tax persons is presented in Figure 1.3. Note the term "enrolled agent" used therein. This term means an IRS-licensed tax practitioner who has been assigned a CAF number (Centralized Authorization File) by the IRS. Thus, we conclude that the attorney in the above case was dead wrong. He should have been sued for malpractice by those family members who were deprived of their full financial share of the estate. Attorney commissions come off the top. Some attorneys are just too cocky and too arrogant. Those who are tend to do more harm than good.

Form 706	U.S. ESTATE . . . TRANSFER TAX RETURN	
Part 1 - Decedent & Executor		
Part 2 - Tax Computation		
Part 3 - Elections by Executor		
PART 4 - General Information & Authorization		

Authorization to act as the estate's representative before the IRS, and to make written or oral presentation (thereto)... by an attorney, accountant, or enrolled agent.

Name of representative	Address

I declare that I am the ☐ attorney ☐ certified public accountant ☐ enrolled agent... for the executor and prepared this return for the executor. I am not under suspension or disbarment from practice before the Internal Revenue Service

/s/ Signature	CAF No.	Date	Phone No.

16 lines of other information to be provided.

PART 5 - Recapitulation of 15 attached schedules

Separately signed by Executor & by the preparer . . . . ▶ /s/ _____

. . . *under penalties of perjury.* ▶ /s/ _____

Fig. 1.3 - Excerpts from Headportion of Part 4 of IRS Form 706

Church Attorney Switcheroo

We have another bad attorney example for you. The victim was a retired school teacher, widowed, with no children. Her predeceased husband was a small business owner who had been moderately successful in his stock investments. Both he and his wife were devout church goers.

After the husband's death, the wife fumbled with the stock investments. Her fumbling included the proceeds from sale of the decedent's business assets. Observing this, a church friend introduced her to a young woman "financial counselor" who was also a member of the church. The wife placed all of her assets except the home in the hands of this counselor (actually, a stock broker). The wife was 72 years old at the time.

Meanwhile, the wife had a will and a living trust prepared. Her intent was that 50% of her estate (after taxes and expenses) would go to 15 dear friends, and 50% directly to her church. She carefully explained her wishes to the tax person who did her husband's Form 706 and their joint Form 1040 returns for many years. The tax person questioned the motivation of the stock broker. The broker/counselor was getting the wife totally invested in the stock market and in high risk tax shelters (which the wife didn't understand). Subsequently, the wife exchanged her home for a condo-type dwelling in her church's retirement facility.

While in the retirement facility for only 60 days, she had a severe stroke. This left her speech and mental faculties greatly impaired. Upon learning of this, the stock broker contacted an attorney who was a member of the church. The attorney and stock broker, with the church home administrator as a witness, revoked the wife's former will and trust in its entirety. This abruptly cut off all 15 of her closest and dearest friends.

The church attorney substituted a Charitable Remainder Trust (CRT) through which 100% of the estate (just under $2,000,000) went directly to the church. The attorney and broker devised an investment scheme where the CRT distributions took place over a 10-year period. That meant 10 years of attorney commission milkings and 10 years of broker commission churnings.

This was "all legal" because the wife, as trustor of the CRT, was alive at the time. She was conscious enough to mumble "Uh-huh" when asked if she approved of the switchover. She died two days later, without any notice being given to her dear friends.

There's a moral here. Attorneys who are members of the same church as the decedent can engage in disreputable ethics that are no different from nonchurch attorneys. With respect to estates, stock brokers and attorneys are more on the same wavelength than are tax persons and attorneys.

Engineer with Attorney Brother

We still have one more instructional example for you. The decedent, an unmarried man, had a Ph.D. in Nuclear Engineering (majoring in nuclear physics). As an employee of a global engineering corporation, he was sent to various nuclear power plants as a consultant on nuclear fuel rod design, fuel rod handling, reactor shielding, and safety inspections. During his U.S. and foreign assignments, he was frequently exposed to nuclear radiation, much of it at close hand. Gradually, he developed leukemia and died at the age of 52.

Long before his death, he befriended a young family: an engineer with wife and two children. He visited their home frequently, stayed overnight on occasions, and even went on vacations with them. As the years went by, he was getting sicker and sicker from leukemia. After release from the hospital one time, and in discussions with his tax preparer, he had a will and living trust drawn up. Although his brother was an attorney, he sought the services of an attorney elsewhere. He, as an engineer, and his brother, as an attorney, never saw eye-to-eye on financial and estate matters. In the end, he designated the wife of his engineer friend to be the executor of his estate, and also to be the trustee of each of two $30,000 educational trusts for his friends' two children (his "nephew" and "niece"). He also directed that his appointee (an energetic, educated woman) be entitled to the full statutory executor fee. After all taxes and expenses were paid, his residual estate would go to his brother and two sisters equally. All three heirs were foreign citizens.

The decedent's gross estate totaled approximately $2,068,000. This consisted of his residence ($450,000), a private yacht ($250,000), a yacht moorage ($100,000), mutual funds ($625,000), life insurance ($500,000), art collection ($75,000), and bank accounts ($68,000). After deductions, expenses, and the exemption allowance, his transfer tax (federal and state) was $315,000 . . . an effective 15% death tax rate.

```
Internal Revenue Service
Cincinnati, OH 45999              Date of issue: _____


                 Estate Tax Closing Document
                    NOT a bill for tax due


    Addressee: Preparer of Form 706
    Estate Name: The decedent
    Social Security Number: _____
    Date of Death: _____

    We have determined the following:
                NET ESTATE TAX ....................... $_____
                STATE DEATH TAX CREDIT............... $_____
                GENERATION SKIPPING TAX ........... $_____

    - Please keep this document in your permanent records.
    - Proof of payment in the amount shown above releases you of
      personal liability thereof.
    - We will not reopen this return unless... there is evidence of mis-
      representation of a material fact, a clearly defined
      substantial error, or a serious administration omission.

                              /s/        IRS
                          Chief, Estate, & Gift Tax Program
```

Fig. 1.4 - Abridgment of Estate Tax Closing Document

The executor engaged her tax preparer (the same person who prepared the decedent's Form 1040 returns) to do IRS Form 706 and the two educational trust Forms 1041. Within four months Form 706 was completed and filed with the IRS (at a charge of around $5,000). About two months later, the IRS issued an *Estate*

Tax Closing Document: its formal way of closing all estate tax matters. The format and selected excerpts from such a document are presented in Figure 1.4. Note the finality of the document except for any misrepresentation of a material fact.

In other words, within six months after the decedent's death, the executor had completed and filed Form 706, probated the estate (a nonattorney executor *can* probate legally), received a closure document from the IRS, and began assigning the residual estate to the three foreign heirs. Accomplishing so much in such a short time for a $2,000,000 estate is unheard of in the legal profession.

Upon learning that the Form 706 was prepared by a tax person and not by an attorney, the decedent's brother (a millionaire Swiss attorney) became furious. He engaged a prestigious U.S. law firm to re-examine Form 706, the probate proceedings, and all accounting records maintained by the executor and her tax preparer. The law firm attorneys began threatening to have the executor relieved of her duties and have her $35,000 executor fee invalidated. They also began threatening the tax person with a lawsuit for practicing law. They wanted the case reopened and demanded a $100,000 retainer for their services.

Undaunted, the executor refused. She engaged a separate attorney to quell the law firm and have it accept the IRS's closing document as final. This occurred and she continued as executor.

There you have it!

Our plain message is this. While thinkingly alive, there are many things you can do re estate affairs . . . **without** an attorney. You hire an attorney when you truly need one. You don't hire one to do things that you can do on your own, nor for things that a nonattorney can do.

2

YOUR "GROSS ESTATE"

> Your Gross Estate Will Be Form 706 Probed For: (A) Real Estate, (B) Stocks & Bonds, (C) Notes & Cash, (D) Life Insurance, (E) Joint Property, (F) Other Property, (G) Gifts & Transfers, (H) Trust Powers, And (I) Annuities. These "9 Asset Schedules" Define Your Gross Estate ANYWHERE IN THE WORLD! Very Little Property Of Value, Or Rights To The Enjoyment Of Such Property, Escape The Formidable Corralling Process Of The 40-Page Death Tax Return. Knowing What Is Required On Form 706 Is The NECESSARY PRELUDE For Organizing Your Affairs While Alive. It Is Far Better That You Do This For Yourself, Than Relying On Others.

Over our years of working and living, raising a family and so forth, we accumulate assets and liabilities. The term "assets" refers to items of property and monetary holdings that are readily marketable to third-party (nonfamily) interests. The term "liabilities" refers to those obligations of debt — more than 30 *days* old — that are owed to third-party interests. Taken together, your assets less your liabilities constitute your "net worth." More specifically, however, the IRS focus is on your *Gross Estate*. The magnitude of such estate sets the stage for a whole raft of probings into your financial and property affairs, after death.

One's gross estate changes over the course of time. After the children are grown, the gross estate tends to accumulate more rapidly than it can be consumed. During the rapid buildup period, rarely does one take a serious snapshot of his or her estate. Even when occasional snapshots are made, they do not involve the detailed accounting nor the permanency, when you are no longer around to supervise and manage your own affairs.

When the end of life comes, you have what is then called: a *Transfer Estate*. This is that estate which is no longer being accumulated or consumed by yourself and/or your spouse. It is that which is available — after debts and expenses — for transfer to heirs and others. Before the transfer is consummated, however, a federal transfer tax (otherwise known as an "estate tax" or "death tax") may be imposed. This, then, becomes the ultimate defining moment of your gross estate.

In this what-you-have chapter, therefore, we want to familiarize you with what constitutes your gross estate . . . for death tax purposes. We also want to acquaint you with a rather formidable tax return — **Form 706**: *U.S. Estate and . . . Transfer Tax Return* — that you've probably never seen or thought about before. Rare indeed does a living person give serious thought to the disclosure requirements of Form 706. It is for this reason that we want to present to you an overview of it.

Transfer Tax Imposed

We want you to start off thinking in down-to-earth reality. A federal transfer tax **is** imposed. Whether you transfer a portion of your estate irrevocably during life, or transfer it all after death, a tax is imposed. Before said tax is determined, however, you are allowed certain deductions, exemptions, and credits. What is left after these allowances is subject to tax. It is a *transfer tax*. It is tax on the privilege of transferring money or property gratuitously, to successors who will use it for their own enjoyment.

We know, you've been led to believe that, perhaps, if you set up some kind of exotic-sounding trust, you can avoid taxes, avoid probate, avoid creditors, avoid complicating your estate, and avoid anything and everything that you don't like to do. You can succumb to such fantasies all you want. But you can't avoid the reality that a transfer tax *will be imposed*! The Internal Revenue Code (IRC) does not vanish into cyberspace simply because you are enthralled with the prospects of tax and creditor avoidances through various trust and insurance schemes.

IRC Section 2001(a): *Imposition of Estate Tax*, says succinctly and forcefully—

*A tax is hereby imposed on the **transfer** of the taxable estate of **every decedent** who is a citizen or resident of the United States.* [Emphasis added.]

IRC Section 2501(a)(1): *Imposition of Gift Tax*, says also succinctly and forcefully—

*A tax . . . is hereby imposed for each calendar year on the **transfer of property** by gift during such calendar year by **any individual**, resident or nonresident.* [Emphasis added.]

IRC Section 2601: *Imposition of Generation-Skipping Tax*, says tersely and succinctly—

A tax is hereby imposed on every generation-skipping transfer.

A "generation-skipping transfer" is the transfer of property directly to grandchildren and great-grandchildren. The GST tax is *added onto* that imposed by Sections 2001 and 2501. So, the next time you attend one of those free wealth preservation seminars sponsored by legal, accounting, insurance, and financial firms, keep the above three citations in mind. They and their related sections are valid at least through taxable year 2009. Listen carefully to all of the advantages of the "estate planning" arrangements being proposed. At the opportune moment, pop the ugly question. Nervously . . . and politely, ask—

"If I have a 5 million dollar estate, will the arrangement you propose avoid the transfer tax imposed by Sections 2001, 2501, and 2601 of the Internal Revenue Code?"

You'll become instantly unpopular with the seminar sponsor and his entourage of experts. Similarly with many of the attending guests. You may even be accused of being an IRS spy. Assure the accusers that you are not. You — like all the rest of the attendees — want to avoid as many taxes as you can. Then explain—

"I read a book by some tax guy who claims you can't avoid transfer taxes for estates in the five million dollar and upwards range. Is he wrong?"

Exemption Amounts & Unified Credits

Every taxable estate is allowed a specified exemption amount, depending on the year of death. The term "every estate" means just that. The exemption amount is a separate right of every individual, regardless of marital status. For a married couple, there are two exemption amounts: one for each spouse. There is no sharing or trade-off between spouses. This is because of year-of-death differences in exemption amounts. Death year differences are shown in Figure 2.1 below. Thus, Form 706, previously mentioned, is a **per individual decedent** tax return.

The basic tax law on point is Section 2010: *Unified Credit Against Estate Tax*. Its subsection (a): *General Rule*, reads—

A credit of the applicable credit amount **shall be allowed** *to the estate of* **every decedent** *against the tax imposed by section 2001* [Imposition of Estate Tax]. [See Figure 2.1 for conversions from exemption amounts to equivalent credits.]

For Decedents Dying During -	Exemption Amount	Equivalent Credit Against Tax
2000 & 2001	$ 675,000	$ 220,550
2002 & 2003	1,000,000	345,800
2004 & 2005	1,500,000	555,800
2006, 2007, & 2008	2,000,000	780,800
2009	3,500,000	1,455,800
beyond 2009	??	??
Sec. 2010 - Unified Credit Against Estate Tax Subsec. (c) - Applicable Credit Amount		

Fig. 2.1 - Applicable Exemption Amounts for Estate Tax Purposes

Similarly, Section 2505: *Unified Credit Against Gift Tax*, applies. Its subsection (a): **General Rule**, reads—

*There **shall be allowed** as a credit against the tax imposed by section 2501 [above] for each calendar year [the donor is alive] an amount equal to—*

*(1) the applicable credit amount equivalent to an exemption amount of $1,000,000 for such calendar year, **reduced by***

*(2) the sum of the amounts allowable as a credit to the **individual** under this section for all preceding calendar periods. [Emphasis added.]*

Note that the common term: *Unified*, is used in Sections 2010 and 2505. This commonality often leads to confusion. It is the *tax rates* that are unified; **not** the exemption amounts. The exemption amounts for estate tax purposes are higher than the $1,000,000 fixed amount for gift tax purposes. Nevertheless, by unifying the rates, either exemption amount can be converted to tax dollars for a subtraction credit against the computed tax.

The statutory limit on the exemption amount is prescribed in Section 2010(c): *Applicable Credit Amount.* In general terms, the exemption amount extends from $1,000,000 to $3,500,000 depending on the year of a decedent's death. Before any estate tax applies, the statutory exemption amount is factored in. A tabulation of the specific amounts is presented in Figure 2.1. You might want to glance down the center column there, and pick the exemption threshold that would apply in your case.

The exemption amounts in Figure 2.1 are NOT contingent upon any professionally prepared "estate plan," exotic trust, or insurance arrangement. Whether you have some fancy plan or not, you are entitled to the statutory exemption amounts. Yet, most sponsors of wealth preservation seminars and their expert speakers *imply* — they don't come right out and say so — that the exemptions are the consequence of the particular arrangements that they propose. If you have this belief, you have been misled.

Particularly note in the section titles above, use of the term: *Unified Credit Against . . . Tax.* This term arises from computational technicalities involving mixed life/death use of the exemption amounts. A tentative tax (at graduated rates from 18% up to 45%) is computed first. Then a "credit" corresponding to each exemption amount is applied. We posted in Figure 2.1 the equivalent credits for reducing the tax. We can tell you now that the graduated rate structure flattens out for taxable estates exceeding $2,000,000 (2 million). If the estate tax is not repealed in year 2009 as presently scheduled, Congress has indicated that the maximum rate would be 35% in year 2010 and beyond.

Gross Estate Defined

Regardless of your specific exemption amount, all estate matters and transfers during life have to be fully accounted for at time of death. This involves the process of establishing your gross estate: item-by-item, dollar-by-dollar. This itemization for transfer tax purposes is far more detailed than you ever imagined. Yet, it is the very first step in understanding what you need to do towards organizing your estate for its transfer to others. You can not transfer property which you do not own.

In the most succinct terms possible, your gross estate is defined by Section 2031(a): *Gross Estate; General*, as follows:

*The value of the gross estate of the decedent shall be determined by including to the extent provided for in this part, the value at the time of his death of **all property**, **real or personal**, **tangible** **or** **intangible**, **wherever** **situated**.* [Emphasis added.]

This is an all-sweeping concept: *all property* (real, tangible, intangible, personal) *wherever situated*. The term "all property" means those property items which are marketable to third-party interests at arm's length value. The term "wherever situated" means anywhere in the world! Why, only at death, is such an all-inclusive concept imposed?

Answer: Upon death, one's gross estate is fixed. It cannot be further changed by the decedent who accumulated the estate. It is that moment of finality we all face.

Exactly, what does the Internal Revenue Code have to say about: "all property . . . wherever situated"? You really don't want us to enumerate and explain each of the 92 applicable sections (2001 through 2704), do you?

The simplest official response that we can present is *Part 5 — Recapitulation*, of **Form 706**: *U.S. Estate Tax Return*. Accordingly, we do so in Figure 2.2. You might want to take a moment to read down each of the nine Form 706 schedules listed. The title of each schedule (though abbreviated in some instances) gives you a bird's eye view of what is regarded as your gross estate at time of death.

Form 706	U.S. Estate Tax Return	
Part 5 - Recapitulation		
Schedule	/////////////	Value at Death
///////	**Gross Estate**	///////
A	Real Estate	
B	Stocks & Bonds	
C	Mortgages, Notes, & Cash	
D	Insurance on Decedent's Life	
E	Jointly Owned Property	
F	Other Miscellaneous Property	
G	Transfers During Decedent's Life	
H	Powers of Appointment	
I	Annuities	

Fig. 2.2 - The 9 Gross Estate Schedules on Form 706

Each of the Figure 2.2 schedules is a comprehensive accounting document of its own. A few purely overview comments on each of these nine schedules are essential to understanding your (or your executor's) estate accounting tasks.

Schedule A — Real Estate

The ownership of land (and its appurtenances) is fundamental to any transferable estate. Land is real and fixed. Though its surface may be modified and improved, and buildings erected onto it, land generally is not capable of being consumed or destroyed. Except for defined subsurface mineral, gas, and water rights, one's ownership of land, technically, goes down to the center of the Earth and includes the molten lava.

At any rate, Schedule A of Form 706 requires a descriptive listing and the current market value of all parcels of land owned and used by the decedent. On this point, and for all gross estate schedules, Section 2033 is directly pertinent. The title of Section 2033 is: *Property in Which Decedent Had an Interest*. Its one sentence mandate is—

*The value of the gross estate shall include the value of all property **to the extent of the** [ownership] **interest therein** of the decedent at the time of his death.* [Emphasis added.]

By its very nature, land and its appurtenances is subject to co-ownership and multiple ownership arrangements. This characteristic is more prevalent in real estate holdings than with other forms of a decedent's assets. Hence, the ownership aspects of the decedent must be identified in exact percentages of the total parcel, for proper entry on Schedule A. Generally, if the decedent owns 50% or more of a real estate item, that item is entered on Schedule A. If he owns less than 50%, the item is listed and described on other schedules, such as E, F, G, or H.

If a parcel of real estate is co-owned by the decedent and his spouse, the total professionally-appraised value of the property is entered on Schedule A. Immediately below said entry, an offsetting entry for the surviving spouse is made. Typically, such ownership is 50/50, though it could be non-50/50. For example, the offsetting entry could be—

LESS 50% for spouse's interest.........................<   >

The official instructions to Schedule A of Form 706 say—

Describe the real estate in enough detail so that the IRS can easily locate it for inspection and valuation. For each parcel of real estate, report the [geographic] area and, if the parcel is improved, describe the improvements. For city or town property, report the street or number, ward, subdivision, block and lot, etc. For rural property, report the township, range, landmarks, etc. [Attaching a copy of the recorded legal description of the land is recommended.]

There is a crucial point being made by the above instructions. Of all your gross estate holdings, real estate is the principal target for "inspection and valuation" by the IRS. This is because, in most cases, real estate comprises the dominant dollar value item. For practical purposes, estate tax rates for real estate *start* at 35% to 40%. Consequently, there is temptation to low value real estate rather than fair market value it. The IRS is fully aware of this temptation. That's why it wants to know where the property is, so that it can send its own appraisers out for confirmation.

The more parcels and types of real property that a decedent has, naturally the more complicated his estate affairs will be. It is for this reason that we devote an entire chapter, namely Chapter 8: Culling Real Estate, to ways for organizing one's real "estate."

Schedule B — Stocks, Bonds, Etc.

Officially, Schedule B of Form 706 is titled: *Stocks and Bonds*. By so limiting the title, the implication is that nothing else goes on this schedule whatsoever. But what about mutual funds? And, what about other portfolio assets which are stock-and-bond-like in character? Ownership interests in real estate investment trusts, mortgage backed securities, limited partnership activities, mining exploration undertakings, oil and gas wells, foreign government securities, foreign corporate securities, and a host of other interests in stock and bond derivatives, certainly qualify for inclusion and listing on Schedule B.

For our purposes of identifying asset areas that can be organized, we regard Schedule B as the repository for variable-unit-value assets of the decedent. More collectively, the items listed are intangibles known as *portfolio* assets. Said assets are "intangible" in that they are "pieces of paper" representing fractional interest in real and tangible property, and in entrepreneurial businesses.

The IRS is certainly not going to object if one lists on Schedule B every single variable-unit-value asset that a decedent has. In fact, no other schedule of Form 706 is so adaptable for such items. Furthermore, many estate holders have a very large portion of their wealth in Schedule B-type intangibles. For some, the extent of wealth in Schedule B exceeds that in Schedule A.

The official instructions to Schedule B are exceedingly detailed. Only to give you the flavor of these instructions, we cite just one of its 21 paragraphs, to wit:

List interest and dividends on each stock or bond separately. Indicate as a separate item dividends that have not been collected at death, but which are payable to the decedent or the estate because the decedent was a stockholder of record on the date of death. However, if the stock is being traded on an exchange and is selling ex-dividend on the date of the decedent's death, do not include the amount of the dividend as a separate item. Instead, add it to the ex-dividend quotation in determining the fair market value of the stock on the date of the decedent's death. Dividends declared on shares of stock before the death of the decedent but payable to stockholders of record **on a date after the decedent's death are not includible** *in the gross estate.* [They are includible on Form 1041 which is an income tax return. Form 706 is a transfer tax return.] [Emphasis added.]

In many gross estate situations, the number of entries on Schedule B can range from 5 to 50 . . . to 150! In this event, one or more *Continuation Schedules* is necessary. For simplicity-focusing purposes, Schedule B is where most of the action lies. Accordingly, we have much more to tell you about Schedule B later in Chapter 9: Slimming Portfolio Assets. We regard "slimming" as part of the organization and weeding-out process.

Schedule C — Mortgages, Notes, & Cash

Whereas Schedule B accommodates variable-unit-value assets, Schedule C accommodates fixed-value assets. That is, a Schedule C asset is fixed in terms of number of dollars. There is no $/unit, $/share, or $/contract to be concerned with. The only concern with fixed dollar assets is the effect of monetary inflation (over many years: five or more). However, for Schedule C listings, the effect of inflation is ignored. Account balance values are used.

As to the assets prescribed for Schedule C (Form 706), the instructions say—

List items on Schedule C in the following order:
- *mortgages,*
- *promissory notes,*
- *contracts to sell land,*
- *cash in possession, and*
- *cash in banks . . . and other financial organizations.*

The instructions go on to say—

List on Schedule C:
- *mortgages and notes **payable to** the decedent at time of death.*

***Do not** list on Schedule C:*
- *mortgages and notes **payable by** the decedent at time of death. (If deductible, list them on Schedule K.)*

Mortgages payable **to** the decedent generally arise from self-financing of real estate sales, or from monies advanced in the form of second trust deeds secured by real property. A mortgage is an enforceable instrument which has a face value, an unpaid balance, rate of interest, and date of maturity. Seller-financed mortgages are especially attractive as an organizing endeavor where there are multiple holdings of real estate, of which one or more parcels are sold on the "installment method." Mortgages can be reassigned to one or more of the decedent's heirs without the appraisal, title, and management complexities of real property itself.

Cash holdings in the form of promissory notes, land contracts, savings accounts, certificates of deposit, money market funds, and checking accounts often comprise a very significant portion of a decedent's estate. The liquidity of such assets makes them the ideal focus for serious estate-organizing effort. We revisit this effort in Chapter 7: Goals to Pursue.

Schedule D — Life Insurance

Officially, Schedule D (Form 706) is titled: ***Insurance on the Decedent's Life.*** Said insurance is treated as an asset of the decedent. Before death, each life insurance policy, ordinarily, has a determinable cash value. At the instant of death, its cash value is substantially magnified. It is for this reason that the headnote instruction to Schedule D says, emphatically:

*You must list **all** policies on the life of the decedent and attach a Form 712 for each policy.*

Form 712 is titled: **Life Insurance Statement**. It consists of two parts: (I) ***Decedent-Insured*** (35 lines), and (II) ***Living Insured*** (32 lines). The "statement" provides information on the face amount of the policy, amount of one sum proceeds, value of proceeds as of date of death (if not payable as one sum), name of beneficiaries, and name of the policy owner. Other instructions to Form 712 say—

If decedent is not owner, attach copy of [insurance] application. If policy has been assigned [to other than the decedent or his estate], attach a copy of the assignment.

Schedule D is the direct consequence of IRC Section 2042: ***Proceeds of Life Insurance***. The gist of which is—

The value of the gross estate shall include the value of all property—

*(1) **Receivable by the executor** . . . to the extent of the amount . . . as insurance under policies on the life of the decedent.*

*(2) **Receivable by other beneficiaries** . . . [if] the decedent possessed at his death any of the incidents of ownership [of the policy on his life], exercisable either alone or in conjunction with any other person [or entity].*

To include or not include the proceeds of life insurance on Schedule D (Form 706) has been a controversy of long standing between the IRS and the insurance industry. This controversy arises because Irrevocable Life Insurance Trusts (ILITs) are marketed as being excludable from gross estates. The IRS has argued successfully that if proceeds from a life insurance trust are used to pay the estate tax, or any other taxes, debts, or charges against the decedent's estate, such proceeds **are** includible.

Schedules E & F — Other Property Items

Schedules E and F are titled, respectively: *Jointly Owned Property*, and *Other Miscellaneous Property Not Reportable Under Any Other Schedule*. Schedule E is arranged in two parts (jointly owned with spouse, and jointly owned with others), whereas Schedule F starts off with three probing Yes-No questions. Both Schedules E and F are regarded as catchalls for those assets that don't expressly qualify for inclusion on Schedules A, B, and C: real estate, stocks and bonds, and cash.

Part 1 of Schedule E: *Qualified Joint Interests Held by Decedent and His or Her Spouse*, overlaps with those items in Schedules A, B, and C. The term "qualified" spousal interests applies when an item is held as:

- Tenants by the entirety, or
- Joint tenants with right of survivorship

As such, once the spousal property assets are itemized and totaled, one-half (or 50%) is excluded from the decedent spouse's gross estate. If several significant assets are so held, listing them in Schedules A, B, and C, then subtracting 50%, is more practical than listing them in Part 1 of Schedule E.

Part 2 of Schedule E directs attention to "all other" surviving co-tenants. The form is set up for listing separately the name, address, and percentage ownership of each co-tenant. For each property so identified (and full valued), the *inclusion percentage* of the decedent is stated and applied to the full value. Otherwise the 750-word instructions say in part—

If you believe that less than the full value of the entire property is includible in the gross estate for tax purposes, you must establish the right to include the smaller value by attaching proof of the extent, origin, and nature of the decedent's interest and the interest(s) of the decedent's co-tenant or co-tenants.

Co-tenancy property tends to be that which is inherited, held in trust, acquired in joint ventures, shared in a partnership, or held for investment (such as rental real estate). Where there are multiple properties and multiple co-tenants, the result often is extreme complication when gross estating a decedent's Form 706. This is because the tracing of each co-owner's contribution of money (or its equivalent) is fraught with poor records.

The headportion of Schedule F: *Other Miscellaneous Property*, directs specific attention to—

- Articles of artistic or collectible value,
- Bonus or awards to other than decedent as a result of decedent's employment or death, and
- Access to a safe deposit box.

Below the Yes-No safe deposit box question, instructions say—

If any of the contents of the safe deposit box are omitted from the schedules in this return, explain fully why omitted.

In other respects, Schedule F is a pure catchall for extraneous forms of assets which decedents and others are often unaware that they have. A listing of the types of items commonly involved is presented in Figure 2.3. The general idea behind Figure 2.3 is that nothing is to be omitted from Form 706 (if it has a value of $100 or more per item). Articles of artistic or collectible value are a "homing beacon" to the IRS. Why not purge them from your estate while alive?

Schedule G — Transfers During Life

Without question, Form 706 is THE most exhaustive tax return ever prepared for an individual. No asset can be omitted if the decedent had even the remotest of ownership interest in, or strings attached to, during-life transfers. The instructions to Schedule G: *Transfers During Decedent's Life*, make the point clear:

All transfers (other than outright transfers for full and adequate consideration and bona fide sales) made by the decedent **at any time during** [his/her] **life** *must be reported on Schedule G regardless of whether you believe the transfers are subject to tax.* [Emphasis added.]

Sched. **F**	Other Miscellaneous Property	Form **706**

1. **Articles of artistic or collectible value**	☐ Yes ☐ No	
2. **Bonus or award to spouse or other**	☐ Yes ☐ No	
3. **Access to a safe deposit box**	☐ Yes ☐ No	

Marital deduction property from predeceased spouse

☐ Debts due decedent	☐ Proprietorship business(es)	☐ Insurance on life of another

● Partnership interests	● Closely-held corporations

- Claims	- Judgments	- Farm machinery
- Refunds	- Trust funds	- Farm products
- Rights	- Automobiles	- Recreational vehicles
- Royalties	- Household goods	- Reversionary interests
- Leaseholds	- Personal effects	- Remainder interests

Fig. 2.3 - Range of Items Includible on Schedule F (706)

This instruction requires that the decedent's executor rummage back many years into the decedent's prior life. This process is time consuming, frustrating, and often encounters strong resistance. It can anger and cause noncooperation by those who want to secrete any special favors to them by the decedent.

Other instructions to Schedule G specify five specific types of transfers that must be included. These are—

(1) Certain gift taxes — Enter the total value of the gift taxes that were paid by the decedent or the estate on gifts made by the decedent or the decedent's spouse within three years before death [Section 2035(b)].

(2) Other transfers within three years before death — Include only the following (as per Section 2035(a)):
• any transfer by the decedent with respect to a life insurance policy within 3 years before death.

• *any relinquishment or transfer of a power of appointment within 3 years before death, if the power would have been includible in the gross estate had the decedent continued to possess it until death.*

• *any transfer within 3 years before death of a retained life estate, reversionary interest, or power to revoke, etc., if the life estate, interest, or power would have been included in the gross estate had the decedent continued to possess it until death.* [These matters are generally opaque with legalese.]

(3) Transfers with retained life estates — These are transfers in which the decedent retained the right to designate the person or persons who will possess or enjoy the transferred property, or the income from the transferred property if the transfer was made [Section 2036].

(4) Transfers taking effect at death — A transfer that takes effect at the decedent's death is one under which possession or enjoyment can be obtained only by surviving the decedent.

(5) Revocable transfers — These are transfers in which the enjoyment of the transferred property was subject at decedent's death to any change through the exercise of a power to alter, amend, revoke, or terminate.

Not much can escape the asset probings of Schedule G. Special rules and tax forms apply when transferring items of value to family members, business associates (as in corporations or partnerships), into trust, or by other "insufficient consideration" means. Convincing documentation of the authenticity of the transfers must be attached.

Schedules H & I — Powers & Annuities

Schedules H and I are titled, respectively: *Powers of Appointment*, and *Annuities*. A "power of appointment" is the right of a decedent to enjoy all or part of the property of someone else which is in trust, under contract, or sequestered by insurance or other arrangement. An "annuity" is a contract for payments over a period of time referenced to the decedent's death. Any power or annuity exercisable in favor of the decedent **is included** in his estate. Instructions accompanying both schedules are explicit on this point.

Instructions to Schedule H say, in part—

Include in the gross estate: (1) The value of the property for which the decedent possessed a general power of appointment on his or her death; and (2) The value of property for which [the decedent] *exercised or released the power before death by disposing of it in such a way that it would* [otherwise be treated] . . . *as a retained life estate, a transfer taking effect at death, or a revocable transfer.*

*A power is **not** includible in the gross estate **if** the decedent **released the power completely** and the decedent held no interest in or control over the property.* [Emphasis added.]

Similarly, for Schedule I the instructions say, in part—

Include in the gross estate the value of any annuity that: (1) Is receivable by a beneficiary following the death of a decedent by reason of surviving the decedent; or (2) Is payable to the decedent . . . for life . . . or for any period that did not in fact end before the decedent's death.

These rules apply to all types of annuities, including pension (profit-sharing, stock bonus) plans, individual retirement arrangements (IRAs), and purchased commercial annuities.

It should be obvious by now that very little property of value, or rights to the enjoyment of such property, escapes the corralling arm of Form 706. No matter what you have accumulated or have tried to preserve during life, it is **all** resurrected at time of death.

Other Items on Form 706

Schedules A through I — the nine asset schedules — comprise the "heavy duty" items on Form 706. These schedules must be tackled and valued first. If the aggregate value of all of these schedules exceeds $1,000,000 corresponding to the years listed in Figure 2.1, Form 706 becomes a mandated filing. When this happens, other items on Form 706 must be addressed.

Preceding Schedule A (Real Estate), there is a series of entry spaces, questions, checkboxes, and requests for general information. These items are arranged as follows:

Part 1 — *Decedent and Executor*
Part 2 — *Tax Computation*
Part 3 — *Elections by the Executor*
Part 4 — *General Information*
Part 5 — *Recapitulation* [of Schedules A through I, and J through U]

Following Schedule I (Annuities), other schedules appear. These are:

J — *Funeral and Administrative Expenses*
K — *Debts of the Decedent*
L — *Net Losses During Administration*
M — *Bequests to Surviving Spouse*
O — *Charitable Gifts and Bequests*
P — *Credit for Foreign Death Taxes*
R — *Generation-Skipping Transfer Tax*
U — *Conservation Easement Exclusion*

(There are no Schedules N, Q, S, and T.) Schedules J, K, and L are expense deductions; Schedules M and O are bequest deductions; Schedules P and U, if applicable, provide additional reductions to your taxable estate.

The point that we are getting at is this. Unless you give serious thought ahead of time, the Form 706 process can be complicated, costly, and frustrating. With only a modest amount of forethought and dedication, Form 706 can be turned into an instructional and highly beneficial experience . . . while you are alive.

3

VALUATION TECHNIQUES, ETC.

We Know, It's A "Real Pain" To INVENTORY (Item By Item) And FAIR MARKET VALUE Your Gross Estate While Alive. Nevertheless, The First Step In Doing So Is To Categorize Your Marketable Assets Into Tailored Categories Such As: (1) Real Estate, (2) Portfolio Holdings, (3) Cash On Hand, (4) Business Interests, (5) Vehicles, (6) Equipment & Tools, (7) Household Items (Over $100 Each), (8) Artistry & Intrinsics (Over $1,000 Each), (9) Rare Collections, (10) Co-Ownership Interests . . . And So On. Valuation Techniques Include: (a) Comparable Sales, (b) Professional Appraisals, (c) Regulatory Formulas, And (d) "Gut Feel" Estimates.

In the preceding chapter: Your "Gross Estate," we basically only defined such an estate. As we tried to explain, your gross estate is more than your personal residence, a few stocks and bonds, a bank account or two, and any business (ownership) interests you may have. Your gross estate is more than just what you have; it is the VALUE — the fair market value — of what you own. Do you have any idea of the realistic present value of your total estate?

Tax valuing your gross estate is not statutorily required until you die. Then, professional appraisers are called to the scene to itemize and value each and every potential marketable asset belonging to you. Professional reports are provided to your executor, who must organize them into Form 706 Schedules A through I that we discussed in Chapter 2. IRS Form 706, recall, is short-titled: *U.S. Estate Tax Return*.

Because full and accurate valuation is not required until one's demise, very few taxpayers voluntarily undergo the tasks on their own. Voluntarily doing so ahead of time — at least once or twice while "thinkingly alive" — will prove invaluable. By directly experiencing the techniques and efforts on your own, you'll make the tasks for your executor much easier, and professional fees, which are often quite costly, will be saved.

Accordingly, in this chapter we want to acquaint you with the valuation techniques and the probing efforts required by IRS regulations. The leadoff such regulation is § 20.2031-1: *Valuation of Property — General*. This general regulation is followed by others that, more or less, follow the sequence of Schedules A through I of Form 706. We point out, however, what appears to be an anomaly in the regulations. There is no one regulation specifically devoted to real estate. There are two reasons for this silence. One, valuation of real estate can be highly opinionated. And, two, there are so many different kinds of real estate holdings that no single valuation technique is recognized across the entire U.S. Even so, applicable regulations can be helpful in that they go beyond the wording prescribed in the federal estate tax laws themselves.

Statutory Overview

Before citing any regulations pertinent to valuation techniques, we should overview (very briefly) the estate tax laws that apply. There are 17 such laws, namely: IRC Sections 2031 through 2046. Including their various subsections, we list the 17 sections for you in Figure 3.1. Skim reading this figure will provide direct insight into what your executor will be up against, upon your demise.

On page 2-6 previously, we quoted the entire subsection 2031(a): *Gross Estate — General*. To refresh your recall, its opening phrase reads—

*The **value** of the gross estate of the decedent **shall be determined** by including . . .* [Emphasis added.]

Nothing in this subsection tells you how to value your gross estate.

It tells you only what to include, namely, *all property, real or personal, tangible or intangible, wherever situated.*

Section	Title	Sub-Sections
INTERNAL REVENUE CODE (IRC)		
Subtitle B - Estate & Gift Taxes		
Subchapter A - Estates of Citizens or Residents		
Part III - GROSS ESTATE		
2031	Definition of Gross Estate	a,b,c,d
2032	Alternate Valuation	a,b,c,d
2032A	Valuation of a Certain [Realty]	a,b,c,d,e,f,g,h,i
2033	Property Decedent Had Interest	-
2034	Dower or Curtesy Interests	-
2035	Gifts Within 3 Years of Death	a,b,c,d,e
2036	Transfers With Retained Life Estate	a,b,c
2037	Transfers Taking Effect at Death	a,b
2038	Revocable Transfers	a,b
2039	Annuities	a,b
2040	Joint Interests	a,b
2041	Powers of Appointment	a,b
2042	Proceeds of Life Insurance	-
2043	Transfers for Insufficient Consideration	a,b
2044	Certain [Marital Deduction] Property	a,b,c
2045	Prior Interests	-
2046	Disclaimers (Also Sec. 2518)	a,b,c

Fig. 3.1 - Tax Code Sections Requiring Gross Estate Valuation

The nearest "how" instruction is in subsection 2031(b): *Valuation of Unlisted Stock and Securities.* In selected part, this subsection goes on to say—

The value thereof shall be determined by taking into consideration . . . the value of stock or securities of corporations engaged in the same or similar line of business which are listed on an [established public] *exchange.*

This valuation technique is commonly known as **comparable sales**. This technique is used extensively by professional appraisers when no exact match of actual sales can be found.

Subsection 2031(c): *Land Subject to a Qualified Conservation Easement* provides no valuation guidance whatsoever. Its 900 words (or so) focus primarily on definitions such as "qualified land," "conservation easement," the exclusion amount (up to $500,000), and "debt-financed property."

The 4,000 word (or so) Section 2032A: *Valuation of Certain Farm, Etc., Real Property*, presents some techniques regarding farms and closely held business interests. Paragraph (7) of subsection 2032A(**e**): *Method of Valuing Farms* and paragraph (8) thereof: *Method of valuing closely held business interests* are specific but very complex. For example, paragraph (7)(A) says—

> *The value of a farm . . . shall be determined by dividing (i) the excess average annual gross cash rental for comparable land . . . in the locality of such farm, over the average annual State and local real estate taxes for such comparable land by (ii) the average annual effective interest rate for all new Federal Land Bank loans . . . for the 5 most recent calendar years.*

In all other "valuation method" respects, the tax laws are silent. Of those laws listed in Figure 3.1, all of the following sections have the common opening phrase:

> *The value of the gross estate shall include . . .*

No method of inclusion is prescribed. The Figure 3.1 sections using this same phrase are: 2033, 2034, 2036, 2037, 2038, 2039, 2041, 2042, and 2044. Thus, our obvious point is that, for estate valuation purposes, one must resort to the pertinent regulations.

"Fair Market Value" Defined

Regardless of when you may die, the value of almost every item of property that you own has some fair market value (FMV). The exceptions are memorabilia and worn out and damaged items, Otherwise, how is the FMV of your property determined?

To shed light on this term, we call forth IRS Regulation 20.2031-1(b): *Valuation of Property in General.* This is an informative but quite lengthy regulation. Consequently, we are going to take only pertinent excerpts from it, namely:

The fair market value is the price at which the property would change hands between a willing buyer and a willing seller, neither being under any compulsion to buy or to sell and both having reasonable knowledge of relevant facts. [Said]*value . . . is not determined by a forced sale price. Nor is* [it] *. . . to be determined by the sale price of the item in a market other than that in which such item is most commonly sold to the public, taking into account the location of the item wherever appropriate. Thus,* [it is] *. . . the price at which the item or a comparable item* **would be sold at retail**. *. . . All relevant facts and elements of value as of the applicable valuation date shall be considered in every case . . . for each unit of property.* [Emphasis added.]

The key point in this regulatory definition of FMV is *retail price*. It is not some wholesale or bargain price. For example, suppose you have an automobile. Its FMV for gross estate purposes would be the price for which an auto of the same or approximately same description, make, model, age, and condition could be purchased by a member of the general public. It is *not* the price for which the particular auto would be purchased by a dealer in used cars. Nor is it the price that a family member would pay to take it off your hands.

Other excerpts from the above subregulation state:

Livestock, farm machinery, harvested and growing crops must be itemized and valued separately. Property shall not be valued at which it is assessed for local tax purposes unless that value represents its fair market value. The value of items of property which are held for sale in the course of a business generally should be reflected in the value of the business.

Regulation 20.2031 is titled: **Definition of gross estate; valuation of property.** It consists of these nine subregulations:

20.2031-1: Valuation of Property (General)
20.2031-2: Valuation of Stocks and Bonds
20.2031-3: Valuation of Interests in Businesses
20.2031-4: Valuation of Notes
20.2031-5: Valuation of Cash on Hand or on Deposit
20.2031-6: Valuation of Household and Personal Effects
20.2031-7: Valuation of Annuities, Life Estates
20.2031-8: Valuation of Certain Life Insurance
20.2031-9: Valuation of other Property

We quoted above part of subregulation -1, and we'll touch on others as we go along. We just want you to be aware that there are applicable IRS regulations for valuing any and all property includible in your gross estate. The sole exception is real estate. In the listing of nine subregulations above, do you see the term "Real Estate" mentioned?

The Problem with Real Estate

The valuation problem with real estate is that there is so much of it. There are all kinds of it: raw land, farm land, timber land, mineral land, water front land, rural land, suburban land, urban land, etc., etc. There are so many uses for it: residential, commercial, industrial, farming, mining, drilling, recreational, charitable, government, and public accesses. There are all kinds, shapes, and uses throughout the world. As a consequence, the valuation of real property is a local technique where there is no national standard of measure.

Incidentally, the term "real estate" is dictionary defined as—

Land owned as property along with its natural resources and any permanent buildings (and structures) on it.

A "building" is normally thought of as a structure that is habitable by human beings, whereas a "structure" is inhabitable. For example, a boathouse might be a building whereas a boat dock would be a structure. A boathouse or boat dock in Seattle, WA would FMV differently from the identical size and shape in Miami, FL. The point here is that the precise geographical location of real estate is crucial to its valuation results. Such is the well worn theme of all realty agents: *Location, location, location.*

Many persons have much of their ownership and wealth in real estate. The most common form is a personal residence, a second home (perhaps), and a vacation dwelling (maybe). Other realty holdings may include residential rentals, commercial buildings, storage and warehouse structures, natural resources (timber, oil, gas, gravel, minerals), fishing ponds, golf courses, mountain tops, and so on. Speaking of mountain tops, how would you appraise a land-locked 1-acre parcel of scrub land in the foothills with no view and no nothing? It was won in a church raffle raising money for young missionaries.

Answer: You find its latest property tax assessment card and go from there.

All accessible land in the U.S. is surveyed, partitioned into parcels, and account numbered for local property tax administration purposes. The account number is often officially identified as: *Assessor's Parcel Number* (APN) and carries a series of digits such as 393-33-023. The "393" may represent the *Assessment District* in the county where the property is located; the "33" may represent the *Map Number* for that district; and the "023" may represent the actual parcel number on that map. *Notification of Assessed Value* cards are sent out once a year for the official assessment date. Said date usually is either January 1st or July 1st, depending on local practice. A depiction of such a card and its information is presented in Figure 3.2. Every parcel of property that you own or co-own will have a separate assessment card of its own. Do you have a current file of these cards for each parcel of real property you own? If not, do you know how to request them from the County Assessor's Office?

The Figure 3.2 assessment card is only a starter. What you particularly need is the *title deed* to each parcel of property in your holding. The deed describes the land with surveyor's precision and becomes a legal document should boundary line disputes arise. Title deeds are recorded in the official records: *Recorder's Office*, of the county where the property is physically located. If you don't already have the title to each of your properties, you must obtain each and have them in your file of very important papers. In one sense, organizing your gross estate starts earnestly when you have your current assessment cards and recorded title deeds in your possession.

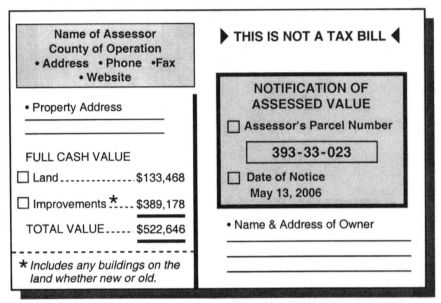

Fig. 3.2 - Example Format of "Assessed Value Notification" to Realty Owners

Above all, do not give your property deeds to an attorney, or seal them in a safe deposit box at a bank. Keep them in a loose-leaf binder, well marked, in a convenient filing location at home. They have no theft value and cannot be sold for cash. Their primary value is the official APN which is seldom memorized.

Website Search for Comparables

Once you have identified and title verified every parcel of realty that you own, the next step is to determine each parcel's FMV. As you already know, the value of real estate is influenced by physical factors within the property itself, and by economic factors exterior to the property. And there may be other factors such as "character" of the neighborhood, scenic views, vicinity of schools and churches, and the roads and streets leading to and from your property. These are the kinds of factors that a professional appraiser would observe and comment on.

For valuation purposes while alive, what is your best (and least expensive) approach? We believe it to be: *Website Searching.* All major real estate brokerage and mortgage lending institutions maintain a website. They have full access to all publicly listed sales of real estate in your area. Select a reputable real estate agency, look up its website, access it, and go from there. Follow the instructions for getting information on: *Comparable Sales in Area.* Type in your address, zip code, tax assessing county, age of home, its living area (in square feet), lot size, and any other details requested. In due course, you'll get one or more screen displays citing sale dates and radial distances from your home (or other property that you have designated). As an example of the kind of printout that you might obtain is presented in Figure 3.3.

Editorial Note: The data presented in Figure 3.3 are actual sales figures for a complex of condos in an upscale ocean view area of California. No real addresses are shown, though said addresses are on the true website.

Assuming that the age, materials of construction, and lot size of the Figure 3.3 sales are all comparable, how would you "compute" the valuation of your property?

Simple. Compute on the basis of sales dollars per square foot (sf) of living area. Using the Figure 3.3 data, each comparable's dollars per square foot would be—

$$\text{Sale 1} = \frac{\$1,400,000}{1,567 \text{ sf}} = \$ \ 893/\text{sf} \ \Big\}$$

$$\text{Sale 2} = \frac{\$1,260,000}{1,202 \text{ sf}} = \$1,048/\text{sf} \ \Big\} \quad \$850/\text{sf}$$
$$\text{Average}$$

$$\text{Sale 3} = \frac{\$1,265,000}{2,073 \text{ sf}} = \$ \ 610/\text{sf} \ \Big\}$$

Thus, for the target property in Figure 3.3 having a living area of 1,055 square feet, its computed/estimated valuation would be:

$850/sf x 1,055 sf = $897,000

Website of Local Real Estate Agency	Home Page, Etc.

Subject Property for Value Search

☐ Address, ZIP, County _____

• Year built: 1990	• Bedrooms: 2
• Lot Size: Condo	• Bathrooms: 2
• Living Area: 1,055 sq/ft	• Other: _____

COMPARABLE SALES IN ZIP CODE AREA

SALE 1	Address, ZIP, County (Radius: 0.45 mile)	
Date: 7/13/2005	Lot Size: condo	Bedrooms: 2
Price: $1,400,000	Living Area: 1,567 sq/ft	Bathrooms: 2

SALE 2	Address, ZIP, County (Radius: 0.19 mile)	
Date: 3/04/2006	Lot Size: condo	Bedrooms: 2
Price: $1,260,000	Living Area: 1,202 sq/ft	Bathrooms: 2

SALE 3	Address, ZIP, County (Radius: 0.38 mile)	
Date: 4/22/2006	Lot Size: condo	Bedrooms: 2
Price: $1,265,000	Living Area: 2,073 sq/ft	Bathrooms: 2

DISCLAIMER re accuracy of data. No warranty, express or implied. Public record data only.

Fig. 3.3 - Edited Value Printout for Condo Sales in Southern California

Valuing real property by means of Internet searching is so practical these days. It is so, for one very special reason. EVERY SALE of real property in the U.S. is recorded in official records of the county where the property is assessed for local tax purposes. Thus, its date of sale, sales price, and description particulars are a matter of public record. Daily updating is routine practice by realty tracking services.

Stocks, Bonds, & Mutual Funds

Another popular form of property holdings involves stocks, bonds, mutual funds, and similar "portfolio"-type accounts. These items are classed generally as "securities," but they include also commodity accounts, option accounts, brokerage accounts, and so on. The idea behind all of these forms of property is to invest an amount of money in the hope that it will appreciate in value; will pay dividends; will pay interest; or will provide other earnings. These items as a group are classed as stock and, where publicly traded, their value (as of a specific date) is relatively easy to obtain. Business newspapers, brokerage firms, and financial websites are readily accessible. For restricted stock (privately traded) or closely-held stock (seldom traded), you'd have to contact an over-the-counter or make-market broker.

The term "bond" addresses specific debt obligations of corporations, governments, municipalities, and public utilities. They are identified by a face amount (principal sum) payable on a fixed due date, at a designated (coupon) rate of interest. For valuing them, contact your source of purchase or issuer by phone, fax, or e-mail. Website searching can always be used.

The term "mutual funds" applies to the pooling of money by many investors into a diversity of stocks, bonds, securities, commodities, and realties. Ownership is by shares (and fractional shares) in a specific fund with a specific objective. Typically, a mutual fund will provide periodic and transactional statements to its shareholders . . . with share values thereon. Most mutual fund managers, upon request (and maybe a small fee), will provide valuation statements for specific dates.

In all cases above, any accrued — but unpaid — interest, dividends, or capital gains to date of valuation should be ascertained and included in your value listings.

The above techniques may seem reasonable enough for during-life valuation assignments. But the IRS, at time of death, refines the techniques still further. Its Regulation § 20.2031-2(b): *Valuation of stocks and bonds*; *based on selling prices*, states—

If there is a market for stocks or bonds on a stock exchange in an over-the-counter market, or otherwise, the mean [average] between the highest and lowest quoted selling prices on the valuation date is the fair market value per share or bond. If there were no sales on the valuation date but were sales on dates within a reasonable time both before and after the *valuation date, the fair market value is determined by taking a **weighted average** of the means between the highest and lowest sales on the nearest date before and the nearest date after the valuation date.*

And so on for another 3,500 regulatory words, subregulationed:

-2(c): Based on bid and asked prices.
-2(d): Based on incomplete selling prices.
-2(e): Where selling prices do not reflect fair market value.
-2(f): Where selling (or bid and asked) prices are unavailable.
-2(g): Pledged securities.
-2(h): Securities subject to an option or contract to purchase.
-2(i): Stock sold "ex-dividend."

All of this IRS "fussiness" is for one very special reason. The Form 706 valuations are required as of date of death. If one dies at night, over the weekend, or on a holiday (when the securities markets are closed), there's a before and after weighted averaging process to go through. However, for estate organizing purposes while alive, this regulatory detail is not required.

Valuation of Business Interests

The term "business interests" generally refers to an ownership interest in a small business and/or in a closely-held entrepreneurial activity. A "small business" is defined as having gross receipts of $5,000,000 (5 million) or less when averaged over a 3-taxable-year period [IRC Section 448(c)(1)]. A "closely-held" enterprise is an entity (corporation, partnership, or limited liability company) where five or fewer owners control more than 50% of the business (regardless of gross receipts).

As Regulation § 20.2031-3 clearly implies, the valuation of an interest in a business requires great care. One reason for such care is that there is no established market for the buying and selling of small businesses. The second reason for great care is that no two small businesses are realistically comparable. Management style, financial practices, accounting techniques, product and services offered, inventory on hand, workforce in place, etc. differ markedly. The value of *goodwill* (repetitive customer base) is particularly difficult to judge. The valuing of tangible assets (machinery, equipment, vehicles) and accounts receivable (invoices rendered) usually involves a discount factor of 20% or so, to enhance their marketability. The valuing of intangible assets (customer lists, workforce in place, system in place, copyrighted business name, statutory licenses, etc.) requires good acquisition cost records for "give and take" valuation projections.

If the business is a C- or S-type corporation, the past three years of balance sheets (assets and liabilities) when averaged, is called "book value." The net book value becomes a starting point for valuation negotiations. Appreciable items on the balance sheets, such as land, buildings, certain machinery (heavy duty type), and securities generally increase the book value.

Not all business partnerships and limited liability companies keep good balance sheet records. Such businesses tend to be cash starved to the point where book value or net worth is not convincingly documented. As a last resort, such businesses can be FMV valued only through the *liquidation process.* That is, the business is considered dissolved, after which each itemized asset, whether tangible or intangible, is placed on the public auction block for cash. Thereafter, comparable values may be obtained via Internet auction sites, flea markets, "for sale" media, and used equipment dealers.

If the business has *demonstrated earning capacity* over three or more years, then commercial brokerage firms specializing in selling small businesses may be contacted. Pay a consulting fee and have your business appraised by a professional. Its FMV may not be as great as you had self-appraised it.

Valuation of Notes & Foreign Accounts

The term "notes" generally refers to an amount of money (or principal) that you have loaned to others under some form of contract (oral or written) for repayment. The contract specifies the initial principal amount, date of maturing (when note is repaid in full), and annual rate of interest. The *face value* of a note is its amount of unpaid principal plus accrued interest thereon. In some cases, a note may be worth less than its face value. This could happen if the debtor is having verifiable financial difficulties such as insolvency, pending bankruptcy, or property pledged as security is insufficient to satisfy the payback obligation. This is the essence of Regulation § 20.2031-4: *Valuation of notes*.

Valuation of cash on hand, bank balances, foreign accounts, and foreign currency is addressed in Regulation § 20.20311-5. The term "cash on hand" applies not only to green paper cash (U.S. currency) but also to checks payable to you that are undeposited, money orders, and gold and silver coins. Bank balances are those shown on periodic bank statements less checks you have written to creditors that have not cleared your bank.

Foreign accounts whether in foreign securities, gold coins, or foreign currencies must be value stated in terms of the official rate of exchange to U.S. currency from each foreign currency. Convertibility difficulties can justify lower valuations, provided you have documentation on the restrictions imposed.

Valuation of Household & Personal Effects

Regulation § 20.2031-6 states in part that—

*A **room by room itemization** of household and personal effects is desirable. All the articles should be named specifically, except* [those] *which have a value of less than $100 each. Such items* [of less than $100 each] *may be grouped and value estimated in the aggregate.* [Emphasis added.]

There is a special rule for "valuable articles." The above regulation goes on to say (in part)—

If there are . . . articles having marked artistic or intrinsic value . . . in excess of $3,0000 [per article] *(e.g., jewelry, furs, silverware, paintings, etchings, carvings, antiques, rare books, statuary, vases, oriental rugs, coin, stamp, or gun collections) the appraisal by an expert or experts should be sought. . . . This is especially true if any collection of similar articles is* [likely to be] *valued at more than $10,000.*

Our take on the above regulatory wording is as follows. Go through each room in your home including its garage and storage shed (if any). Identify each room and assign it a sequence number. Do the same for any second home or vacation home you may have. Glance around each room carefully and categorize all items and articles there as—

1. Memorabilia (photo albums, diaries, handicraft), cooking utensils (pots and pans), and personal clothing — none of these has any true FMV;

2. Items of less than $100 each aggregated into one estimated gross amount for each room;

3. Ordinary items of more than $100 each but no more than $3,000; identify, list, and guestimate their FMV; or

4. Special articles of more than $3,000 each (jewelry, antiques, paintings, crystal, collections, etc.); identify, list, and get a professional appraisal (in writing). Pay some professional fee money now (while alive) so as to save time and mistakes later when deceased.

The idea we have in mind is portrayed schematically in Figure 3.4. Yes, we know it will be a pain to go through the effort depicted in Figure 3.4 while alive. It's all so easy to pass this effort off to your executor (when you die) who will then pass it off to some attorney who, in turn, will pass it off to some high-fee professional to work up an *Inventory and Appraisement Report* for your estate. Doing some of this effort now will test your resolve to really know what your gross estate is likely to be, before life ends. This foreknowledge can be helpful for simplifying your affairs.

Life Insurance, Annuity Contracts, Etc.

End of life thinking raises a whole new set of valuation issues. These issues pertain to the present (or cash) value of life insurance, life estates, annuity contracts, and remainder and reversionary interests in trust-assigned property. These are all referred to as *limited property interests.* That is, one's ownership interest therein is limited by one's life expectancy. This terminology arises from the use of actuarial (life expectancy) tables and adjustments thereto for other probability factors (such as term of years, joint and survivor arrangements, and reversionary interests in trusts).

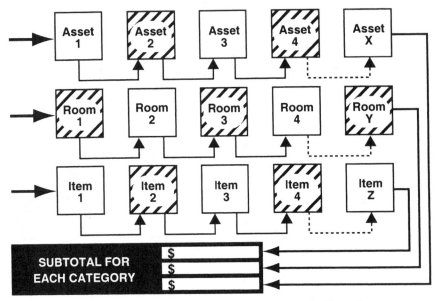

Fig. 3.4 - Systemized Inventory of all Property in Your Estate

In general, the FMV of a limited interest is determined by using an actuarial factor prescribed by the IRS in conjunction with applicable federal rates of interest specified in IRC Section 7520: **Valuation Tables**. For "actuarial factoring," the IRS has provided the following sets of such tables, namely:

- Annuity Tables   **70 pages!**
- Tables for Life Estates, Terms for
  Years, Remainders, and Reversions   **350 pages!**
- Applicable Federal Rates   **230 pages!**

Are you beginning to get the point that we are trying to make?

Our point is that determining the current cash value of any life-expectancy contract is a whole actuarial industry of its own. Neither you nor we can make such determination readily or reasonably. You have no choice other than contacting the insurance company, annuity contractor, trust company, or other financial institution that sold "the contract" to you.

Tailored Asset Categories

At some point in time, you need to pull things together to establish your gross estate for ordinary planning purposes. Tailor your asset categories to your own particular situation. The effort we have in mind is depicted in Figure 3.5.

	Tailored Asset Categories	Date	Value
1	**Real Estate** - *fully owned* with spouse (if any)		
2	**Real Estate** - *co-owned* with other(s) than spouse		
3	Stocks, Bonds, & Mutual Funds		
4	Small Business Interests		
5	Promissory Notes/Accounts Receivable		
6	Foreign Accounts & Currencies		
7	Cash on Hand; Bank Balances, etc.		
8	Vehicles: Autos, Trucks, Boats, Airplanes, etc.		
9	Animals of Value: Horses, Show Dogs, Exotic Pets, Farm Animals, etc.		
10	Machinery, Equipment, & Tools - whether business, farm, or personal		
11	Household Furniture & Furnishings - value exceeding $100 per item		
12	Artistic & Intrinsic Articles - value exceeding $1,000 per item		
13	Marketable Collections - antiques, guns, stamps, rare coins, ceramics, etc.		
14	Uncommon Assets - patents, copyrights, judgements, natural resources		
15	Life Insurance, Annuities, Powers of Appointment, & Limited Property Interests		
16	Inherited/Inheritable Assets - present & future		
X	Anything Else? (Specify)		
	GRAND TOTAL: All of the Above ▶ ▶ ▶ ▶ ▶		$

Fig. 3.5 - Illustrative Asset Categories "Tailored" to Your Estate

While thinkingly alive, we suggest that you start doing so no later than 5 to 10 years into retirement. Disregard (for the time being) the nine asset categories listed on page 2-7 previously. What we are trying to do is to induce you into a frame of mind of wanting to know realistically what your total gross estate is, before your demise. Figure 3.5 is intended to stimulate you in this regard.

We urge that you first read through all of the asset listings shown. Then adapt the list to your own holdings by adding other items to the list, and removing from the list those that are inapplicable. The adding to or removal from process can be done from memory, from observation, or from actual inventory by you or by others within your family.

First, list your own assets . . . then value them later. This is why we show separately a *date* column and a *value* column in Figure 3.5. You are not constrained to valuing everything precisely on the same date. Since you are still alive, the dates and amounts you enter need not be 100% accurate. You want your FMVs to be reasonably close, which they can be when based on intelligent inquiry to family members and friends who have gone through the same process. Also, recourse to media, the Internet, and used property "for sale" sources can be helpful. For articles of intrinsic value (art, jewelry, crystal, ceramics, antiques, collections), professional appraisals are preferred.

By diligently going through an asset listing and valuation processing of your own, one realization should come clearly to mind. That is, you've probably accumulated a lot of "old stuff" and "property clutter" which has no value to family members who otherwise would inherit it. Should this be so, why not get rid of it in a garage sale, offer it to a charity, or have it hauled off to a public dump. This what we call: the *clutter elimination phase* of prudent estate planning.

4

INHERITABLE PROPERTY

After Year 2009, There'll Be A Tectonic Shift In The Tax Basis Rules For Property Acquired From A Decedent. Until Then, The Presently Used STEP-UP In Basis To Fair Market Value At Date Of Death Prevails. The Change Will Be To A CARRYOVER BASIS Regime Using The Decedent's Cost Or Other Basis Adjustments Which, Hopefully, He Or She Has Kept. The Change Involves Treatment Of Inherited Property As A GIFT To Those Individual Persons (Or Their Trusts) Acquiring It. Gift Transfer Accounting Is Used For Establishing Capital Gain Or Capital Loss When Inherited Property Is Subsequently Sold Or Exchanged.

Our concept of what is involved when "Organizing Your Estate" includes the valuation and (tax) basis issues when inheriting property from a predeceased family member. The predeceased member may be one or both of your own parents or other relatives of your parents' generation. For your own children, **you** would be the predeceased member. Thus, the term: *inheritable property* (for our purposes) means that property you acquire from the generation before you, and that which you may pass on to the generation below you. The subject of inheritable property is destined to become more complex because of a new law going into effect in year 2010.

Between now and the end of 2009, the "old rule" of IRC **Section 1014** applies ["IRC" is Internal Revenue Code]. After that year, the "new rule" of **Section 1022** comes into play. You need to know about both of these rules in order to better organize and judge what your eventual distributable estate may be.

Section 1014 is titled: *Basis of Property Acquired from a Decedent.* This is a 2000-word tax law arranged into subsections (a): *In General,* through (f): *Termination* (of Section 1014). Section 1022, in turn, is officially titled: *Treatment of Property Acquired from a Decedent Dying After December 31, 2009.* This tax code section consists of approximately 3,500 words arranged into eight subsections: (a) through (h): *Regulations.* We feel compelled to introduce these two tax laws to you. We feel this way because they comprise a new dimension to estate organizing that you may not have thought about before.

A point to note here is that one's gross estate and his/her distributable estate comprise two quite different monetary values. This can create some estate planning uncertainty. In Chapters 2 and 3, we explained what constitutes your gross estate. For your — and your children's — inheritable property, we need to discuss the distributable estate of any predecedent from whom property may be received. Such is our intention in this chapter.

Page 2 of IRS Form 706

The best way to explain a predecedent's distributable estate is Item 5 on page 2 of Form 706: *U.S. Estate (and . . . Transfer) Tax Return.* There is no distinctive official caption at Item 5. This item is simply one of 16 separate line items comprising **Part 4 — General Information**, on pages 2 and 3. However, if edited, its caption would be—

Individuals, trusts, or other estates who receive property from this estate.
  • *Do not include bequests to surviving spouse nor bequests to charitable entities, as such bequests are deductible elsewhere from the gross estate.*

More specifically, Item 5 comprises four columns as follows:

Col. (1) — Name of individual, trust, or estate receiving $5,000 or more

Col. (2) — Tax identifying number [SSN or EIN]
Col. (3) — Relationship to decedent [by blood, marriage, or adoption; if trust, estate, or friend, so indicate]
Col. (4) — Amount distributed [or to be distributed]

There's a subtle implication in the subcaption to column (1) above. What happens to distributable amounts of less than $5,000 to a beneficiary? Or, to more than one such beneficiary? Or, to various *unascertainable* beneficiaries?

Answer: There's a footnote to column (4) that reads—

All unascertainable beneficiaries and those who receive less than $5,000 [total and enter here] ▶ _____

Additionally, the instructions to column (4) read in part that—

The value entered in this column [for each beneficiary receiving more than $5,000] *need not be exact. A reasonable estimate is sufficient. The total of these distributions should approximate the amount of gross estate **reduced by** funeral and administrative expenses, debts and mortgages, bequests to surviving spouse, charitable bequests, and any federal and state estate taxes paid (or payable).* [Emphasis added.]

The less than $5,000 per distributee and the "need not be exact" instruction for those receiving more than $5,000 provides needed wiggle room for computational imprecisions. When dealing with a gross estate in excess of $1,000,000 (1 million) — often far more than this amount — any small number of "errors" is quite acceptable. Realistically, the recognition of "unascertainable beneficiaries" is essential for computational balancing.

From Gross Estate to Inheritors

An "inheritor" is one or more individual persons, one or more trusts created by the predecedent, and, on occasion, the estate of an individual person who may have died before the predecedent estate is settled. The functional path from one's gross estate to his/her inheritors is portrayed in Figure 4.1.

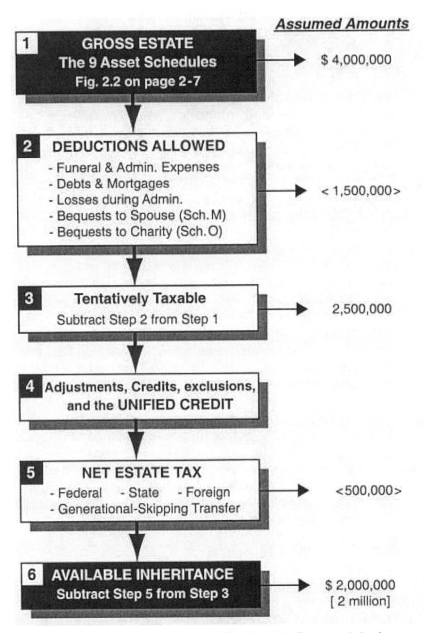

Fig. 4.1 - Form 706 Evolvement of Distributable Estate to Inheritors

We show selected dollar amounts in Figure 4.1 purely for illustrative (functional) purposes. We have sequentially numbered the functional steps for reference purposes. Other than steps 1 and 2, there is no direct correlation with the computational events on page 1 of Form 706: *Tax Computation*.

There are about 20 tax computational lines on page 1 of Form 706. Lines 1 and 2 (corresponding to steps 1 and 2 in Figure 4.1) read precisely as follows:

Line 1 — *Total gross estate less exclusion*
Line 2 — *Total allowable deductions*

The term *less exclusion* in line 1 refers to an "up to" $500,000 off-the-top subtraction from the gross estate for public access across private land for conservation, scenic view points, and historic purposes. While this exclusion is not widely claimed, it is available for wealth estates seeking to minimize the net estate tax. The point we want to make is that the exclusion amount is not an actual subtraction against the gross estate. It is a tax computational matter only. The ultimate distributable estate to inheritors is unaffected by the conservation easement exclusion.

In line 2 (step 2 in Figure 4.1), there are two particular deduction schedules that we want to comment on. The two schedules (on Form 706) are—

M — *Bequests to Surviving Spouse*
O — *Charitable & Public Bequests*

If a decedent has a surviving spouse, the inheritance tax rules are such that the decedent may assign/bequeath his/her *excess taxable estate* to his/her surviving spouse. If there is no surviving spouse, bequests to charitable and public entities can accomplish the same result. That is, for well-off estates, the net estate tax could be reduced to zero (or nearly so) by Schedules M and/or O alone.

What do we mean by our term: *excess taxable estate*? Without Schedules M and/or O, the taxable estate would be that amount which **exceeds** the statutory estate tax exemptions for the year of death. Recall Figure 2.1 on our page 2-4. For death years 2006, 2007, and 2008, for example, the exemption amount is $2,000,000

(2 million). If this amount is directed to individual inheritors, it is TAX FREE! It is tax free to the decedent's estate; it is tax free to the inheritor recipient(s).

What happens to a 2 million dollar tax free transfer of property, when the inheritors decide to sell it, consume it, or transfer it to other family members by gift?

Answer: This is where IRC Sections 1014 and 1022, previously mentioned, come into play. The $2 million is *inherited* tax free, but that's as far as it goes.

The Essence of Section1014

Section 1014 addresses the tax basis of property acquired from a decedent **prior to** year 2010. The term "tax basis" is one's after-tax capital in an item of property that is sold, exchanged, or otherwise disposed of after being inherited. The term is a reference amount for establishing a capital gain, return of capital, or capital lost for **income** taxation purposes. Once the legal ownership of property is in the hands of an inheritor, the estate/transfer taxation rules no longer apply. A new accounting regime applies to that property.

The essence of Section 1014 is its subsection (a): ***In General***, particularly its paragraph (1). Such paragraph reads in part as—

The basis of property in the hands of a person acquiring [it] *from a decedent . . . **shall**, if not sold, exchanged, or otherwise disposed of before the decedent's death by such person, be—*

> *(1)* ***the fair market value*** [FMV] ***of the property at the date of the decedent's death***. [Emphasis added.]

Be reminded that the FMV of a decedent's property item is that which is assigned to it on Form 706. Unless controverted by convincing documentation after death, the FMV amounts shown on the nine asset schedules (A through I) attached to Form 706 are presumed prima facie (at first sight) correct.

The effect of subsection 1014(a)(1) is now what is popularly called: *stepped-up basis*, to an inheritor. Let us illustrate the effect with simple numbers.

Suppose you acquired a $1,000,000 parcel of real estate from one of your deceased parents, or from one of your deceased uncles or aunts (who had no children). Suppose that the decedent had purchased the property for $365,000. You later sell or exchange that property for: Case A — $1,125,000; Case B — $1,000,000, and Case C: $865,000. What are your capital gains and losses therewith? (Disregard all selling expenses.)

Answer—

Case A: $1,125,000 – 1,000,000 basis = $125,000 GAIN
Case B: 1,000,000 – 1,000,000 basis =   ZERO
Case C: 865,000 – 1,000,000 basis = $135,000 LOSS

If a "carryover basis" rule were in effect, instead of the stepped-up basis rule, the corresponding results would be—

Case A: $1,125,000 –   365,000 basis = $760,000 GAIN
Case B: 1,000,000 –   365,000 basis =   635,000 GAIN
Case C: 865,000 –   365,000 basis =   500,000 GAIN

Keep these stepped-up versus carryover basis differences in mind, when we roll out Section 1022 to you.

Modified Stepped-Up Basis

Section 1014(a)(1) is called the general rule for stepped-up basis in inherited property. There are a number of special rules — approximately 12 in all — that modify the general rule. There are too many to discuss here, but we'll cite a few common examples that will convey the gist involved.

The term "modified" means a **reduction** in the full FMV step-up. It is a reduction; not an elimination of the FMV concept. The amount of reduction is proportional to the amount of tax benefits permitted by other tax code sections. These benefits may derive prior to death, at time of death, and up to six months after death. The purpose of modifications is to offset any double tax benefits that otherwise might be allowed the same item of property.

For example, while alive, the decedent purchased a residential rental home for $185,000. Upon renting it, he took the straight line depreciation deduction against the rental income, as allowed by Section 168(b)(3)(B). His cumulative allowable deductions at time of death were $85,000. Thus, his adjusted cost basis in the property was $100,000 (185,000 – 85,000). Yet, at death its FMV was $265,000. In this case, the modified FMV would be $170,000 (265,000 – 85,000). The inheritor still gets a step-up in basis from $100,000 to $170,000; but he gets no double benefits from both depreciation **and** step-up.

Under Section 2032A(a)(2), the decedent owner of a farm or business where land is the estate's predominant asset, may "elect" to discount its FMV up to $750,000. The rules for doing so and its computation are very complex. Nevertheless, if the many acres of land were FMV valued at $1,600,000 (say) and the discount election was $600,000 (say), the inherited basis would be $1,000,000. Compared with the property's acquisition cost of $250,000 (say), the inherited basis would be a substantial step-up.

Under Section 2032(a)(2), a decedent's executor **may elect** an alternate valuation date of six months (to the day) after death. Such an election is attractive where the decedent's property holdings are trending down in value. The election effect is a general reduction in the amount of estate taxes due. See Figure 4.2 for the concept involved. If property is sold by an inheritor between date of death and six months thereafter, the FMV on date of sale becomes the inheritor's tax basis. In this case, the inheritor would experience a capital loss due to the sales commissions and selling expenses involved.

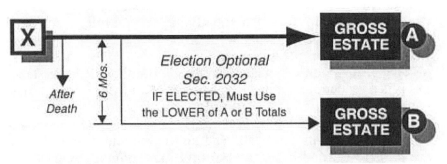

Fig. 4.2 - Election Role of the 6-Month Alternate Valuation Date

Section 1014(b)(6) prescribes a truly unique step-up rule for a husband and wife who own property jointly. (Quoting now) *If at least one-half of the whole of the community interest in such property was includible* [on Form 706]. The nondecedent spouse's one-half is also stepped-up to FMV (at date of death of the decedent spouse). This is probably the best step-up rule of all. The term "community interest" means joint marital property.

Section 1022 "Roll Out"

As previously cited, IRC Section 1022 is officially titled: ***Treatment of Property Acquired from a Decedent Dying After December 31, 2009***. Its approximately 3,500 words are subsection titled as follows:

(a) In General
(b) Basis Increase for Certain Property
(c) Additional Basis Increase for Property Acquired by Surviving Spouse
(d) Definitions and Special Rules
(e) Property Acquired from the Decedent
(f) Coordination with Section 691 [*Recipients of Income in Respect of Decedent*]
(g) Certain Liabilities Disregarded
(h) Regulations [***Ed. Note***: As of this writing (year 2006), the IRS has prescribed no regulations for Section 1022.]

As usual with the tax law wording, its general rule is the reference base from which the interpretation of special rules evolves. In this case, subsection (a) reads in full as follows:

Except as otherwise provided in this section—

(1) *property acquired from a decedent dying after December 21, 2009 shall be treated for the purpose of this subtitle as **transferred by gift**, and*

(2) *the basis of the person acquiring property from such a decedent **shall be the lesser of—***

(A) *the adjusted basis of the decedent, **or***

> *(B)   the fair market value of the property on the date of the decedent's death.* [Emphasis added.]

Do you get the significance of what this general rule is saying?

It is saying that, instead of the prima facie step-up to FMV at time of death (as per Section 1014(a)), the CARRYOVER BASIS of the decedent's property shall prevail. The carryover basis rule is the fundamental premise on which gifts during life are made, and on which tax-free exchanges are made.

Most decedents, by far, die of natural causes. Natural death normally occurs between the ages of 55 and 85. We can tell you from our many years of tax experience with senior citizens that they keep very poor tax basis records. After five years or more of owning a property item, a retiree senior does not know — **and does not care to know** — what his *adjusted basis* is in each of the multiple property items he may own. We postulate, therefore, that the post-2009 carryover basis rules will become increasingly impractical to administer. The IRS has run into this problem previously in gift transfers, personal residence sales, and exchanges of property between spouses incident to divorce.

Historical Commentary

Section 1022 above was enacted on June 7, 2001. It was designated as Public Law 107-16: *Economic Growth and Tax Relief Reconciliation Act of 2001*. This title is political camouflage to disguise the fact that persons of extreme wealth in the U.S. wanted to phase out, terminate, and repeal all vestiges of estate and generation-skipping taxes. Such persons wanted to continue the wealth dynasties of king, monarchs, and monopolists controlling all financial and political power of the day. The Congressional Act itself exposes this disguise in its head summary statement that reads—

> ***Termination of step-up in basis and treatment of property acquired from a decedent after phaseout and repeal of estate and generation-skipping taxes.***

In its own overview of P.L. 107-16, Congress states—

Beginning in 2011, the estate, gift, and generation-skipping transfer taxes are repealed. After repeal, the basis of assets received from a decedent generally will equal the basis of the decedent (i.e., carryover basis) at death. However, a decedent's estate is permitted to increase the basis of assets transferred by up to a total of $1.3 million. The basis of property transferred to a surviving spouse can be increased by an additional $3 million. . . . In no case can the basis of an asset be adjusted above its fair market value.

These modified (stepped-up) carryover rules apply to property acquired by bequest, devise, or inheritance, or by the decedent's estate from the decedent, property passing from the decedent to the extent such property passed without consideration, and certain other property to which the present rules apply. [CCH Standard Federal Tax Reporter, 2006 Vol. 12, page 54,294, Committee Reports on P.L. 107-16.]

Implied in the above is that the year 2010 is expected to be the transition year (from old rules to new rules with regard to inherited property). As things now stand (2006), year 2009 will be the repeal of the estate and generation-skipping transfer taxes. Year 2010 will be a continuation of the gift tax and a "blending" of all three taxes into one common exemption amount of $1,000,000. It is also possible that year 2010 may be full of uncertainty concerning repeal versus reinstatement of the death tax concept. Keep in mind that year 2001 (when P.L. 107-16 was enacted) was the start of an 8-year U.S. presidential cycle. Year 2009 will be the start of another 8-year presidential cycle. Taxation is a political process as much as (in some years more than) it is a revenue process for the functions of government. Federal revenue shortfalls and budget deficits could cause reconsideration of the estate, GST, and gift taxation repeal issue.

With the possibility of death tax reconsiderations in mind, Congress modified its strict carryover basis concept, beginning in 2011. As modified, the basis transfer at death is stepped-up to $1,300,000 FMV for a solo decedent. If married at time of death, a step-up to $3,000,000 is permitted for bequests to surviving spouse. After these two limited FMV step-ups, the strict carryover basis rules apply. We try to depict the changing situation for you in Figure 4.3.

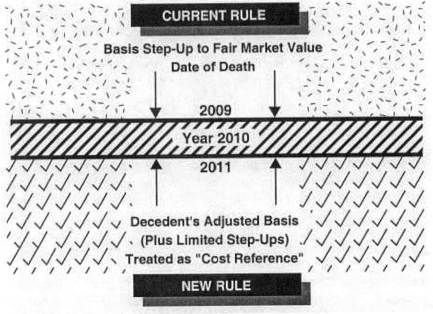

Fig. 4.3 - Prospective Change in Tax Basis for Inherited Property

Think about the prospects ahead for a moment. The entire present regime of estate, GST, and gift taxation will be terminated in year 2010. In its place, only carryover basis rules will apply to property(ies) acquired from a decedent. Can you comprehend fundamentally what this means? Congress gave you a hint in the phrase: *for purposes of this subtitle*, cited in Section 1022(a)(1) above. We think Congress should have been more forthright.

The term "this subtitle" refers to Subtitle A – INCOME TAXES, **which disregards entirely** Subtitle B – Estate and Gift Taxes. Under Subtitle A there is Subchapter O: ***Gain or Loss on Disposition of Property***, Part II – *Basis Rules of General Application* (which includes Section 1022). Altogether Part II consists of 11 separate sections, starting with Section 1011: ***Adjusted Basis for Determining Gain or Loss***, and ending with Section 1023: Cross References. This 11-section package is referenced as: ***Income Tax – Basis Rules***.

From these tax code captions alone, can you recognize what is taking place?

Stated briefly, the death tax (estate, GST, and gift) is being fully replaced by an income tax of the capital gains type. In other words, a 45% tax is to be replaced by a 15% tax. This shift to a lower tax rate is destined to be politically popular in year 2010. The 15% capital gains tax rate has been extended at least through that year. If in 2011 the pre-2001 nominal 20% capital gains rate is resumed, any carryover estate, GST, and gift taxation is to be reset at a maximum of 35%.

No matter what "Tax Reform Act" transpires in 2009, 2010, or 2011, the trend is well focused on replacing the traditional death transfer tax with a garden variety capital gains tax. The proper key for doing so is to document convincingly the decedent's carryover basis in each item of property transferred irrevocably to each heir (or in trust therewith).

Executor Workload Increased

Traditionally, the role of an executor has been to inventory and fair market value a decedent's property at time of his or her death. We see no change in this role. For two reasons. One, the phrase: *The fair market value of the property at the date of the decedent's death* is firmly embedded in Section 1022(a)(2)(B), previously cited. Two, the only practicable (and equitable) way to assign property to inheritees is by its designation in current market dollars: NOT in terms of "adjusted basis."

Beyond the traditional role, we see a greater burden placed on one's executor beginning in 2011. This new burden is the determination of the CARRYOVER BASIS for each item in the decedent's inventory. This burden is self-evident from the statutory terms: *adjusted basis of the decedent* [Sec. 1022(a)(1)(B)], and: *basis increase for certain property* [Sec. 1022(b) and (c)]. This means painstaking effort to resurrect the tax and basis records for each and every item of a decedent's property from its date of acquisition to his/her date of death. If you've ever gone through an IRS audit ("examination," as they call it) where cost or other basis information had to be documented and verified, you know what we mean. If you've not had such an experience, either take our word for it, or dig through your tax basis records on each marketable property item you now own.

Basis recordkeeping on property is probably the most disregarded task of tax life, USA. The IRS knows that basis recordkeeping is a common dereliction of duty by well-meaning taxpayers. Thus, its official policy has silently become: **If no convincing basis records, the basis in that property is zero**. When the zero basis property is sold, the result is all capital gain . . . and income taxed accordingly.

Consequently, we believe that IRS Form 706 will never be eliminated in its entirety. Yes, the estate and generation-skipping tax computations may be curtailed. In their places, new lines and schedules for carryover basis annotations will be prescribed. We foresee Form 706 being extensively revised into a full-blown information return potentially titled as:

Declaration of Decedent's Property and Its Carryover Basis

The carryover basis results will, somehow, have to take into account funeral and administration expenses, debts and mortgages of the decedent, losses (if any) during administration, and adjustments for those liabilities (if any) in excess of basis.

5

CARRYOVER BASIS RULES

> **New Section 1022: Basis Of Property Acquired From A Decedent, Takes Effect When Estate And GST Transfer Taxes "Sunset" On December 31, 2009. In Lieu Of The Former STEP-UP In Basis To FMV, There Are Basis Carryover Rules. The Initial Carryover Is The "Adjusted" Basis" Of Property In The Hands Of The Decedent, Followed By An Aggregate General Basis Increase Of $1,300,000. If Married, An Additional Aggregate Spousal Basis Increase Of $3,000,000 Is Allowed. Each Of These Basis Increases Must Be Apportioned Property-By-Property And Given To Each Heir On A "Transfer At Death" Return.**

Why do we need to tell you about the carryover basis rules for property acquired from a decedent?

Straight answer: Unless you expect to die before January 1, 2010, you will face these rules for your own estate planning and for assisting your parents and others from whom you may inherit property, in their estate arrangements.

The tectonic shift has already been cast in political concrete. Public Law 107-16 (Act of 2001) has added subsection (f): *Termination*, to Section 1014, the step-up basis rule. This termination clause reads quite forcefully as—

This section shall not apply with respect to decedents dying after December 31, 2009.

Simultaneously, P.L. 107-16 added Section 2210: *Termination*, to the *Estate Tax Law*, and Section 2264: *Termination*, to the *Tax on Generating-Skipping Transfers*. Estate and GST taxation — the "death tax" — initiated in 1939, has never been accepted by the populace on fairness grounds. The general rationale has been along the lines that: "We paid income tax on the money we earned to buy the property, so why do we have to pay tax on that property again when we die?"

In P.L. 107-16 — an unprecedented enormous tax reduction Act — there is what is called a *Sunset Provision*. Unless Congress acts to the contrary, all of the 2001 tax reduction efforts are canceled at sunset on December 31, 2010. Then, on January 1, 2011, all prior tax laws are reinstated. Does this mean that the above intended termination provisions for estate and GST taxation will be, themselves, repealed?

No more than you, we have no idea what Congress will do in 2009 and/or in 2010 re property acquired from a decedent. Our sense is that among ordinary taxpayers the estate tax is more adamantly unpopular than is the GST tax. The GST tax arose in 1976 over widespread concerns that wealth dynasties were not paying their fair share of ongoing death taxes down generational lines, once the family monarch or matriarch died. Our sense, therefore, is that some vestiges of the GST tax might be retained. To what extent (if at all) we do not know.

Accordingly, for purpose of this chapter (carryover basis rules) we are going to regard Tax Code Section 1022 re property acquired from a decedent after 2009 as the *wisdom of the decade*. We say this with modest conviction because said section is premised on basis rules with early roots in tax law: *Property Acquired by Gifts*. In other words, inherited property is to be treated as a valuable gift that someday will be sold for full and adequate consideration.

Origin of "Carryover Basis"

Prior to 1921, if a person made a gratuitous gift of property to a family member, the tax basis of that property in the hands of the donee (recipient) was its fair market value (FMV). U.S. income and capital gain taxation was first instituted in 1913. In the seven years that followed, the practice of gifting property among family members became widespread. It was the obviously simple (and legal) way to avoid any capital gain tax whatsoever.

A father could give his son a parcel of land FMV worth $10,000. The son would immediately sell the land for $10,000 . . . and pay no tax. Never mind that the father may have been gifted the land by his older brother, or that the father may have bought the land for $1,000. There was a $9,000 tax gap (10,000 – 1,000) in the gift transaction.

Following World War I (1917-1919), the revenue needs of the U.S. became demanding. It was in this time period that the transfer basis of property by gift was addressed by Congress. The result was what is now Code Section 1015: **Basis of Property Acquired by Gifts** . . . etc. Our annotation "etc." refers to transfers in trust; gifts before January 1, 1921; increased basis for gift tax paid; and approximately 1,200 words of modified basis rules.

For purposes here, subsection 1015(a) is most pertinent. It reads in part as—

If property was acquired by gift after December 31, 1920, the **basis** *shall be the* **same as** *it would be* **in the hands of the donor** *or the last preceding owner by whom it was not acquired by gift, except that if such basis . . . is greater than the* [FMV] *of the property at the time of the gift, then for the purpose of determining* **loss** *the basis shall be such* [FMV]. [Emphasis added.]

This was the original wording enacted in 1920 that remains in effect today. The emphasized phrase: *same as . . . in the hands of the donor* has evolved into the more modern generic term: "carryover basis." That is, the property basis is carried over from the transferor (current owner) to the transferee (new owner). The carryover concept is particularly vital to gratuitous transfers where no real money changes hands, such as at death.

And thus, the introductory wording to Section 1022 (gratuitous basis treatment after 2009) now reads (in part)—

Property acquired from a decedent dying after December 31, 2009 **shall be treated** *. . . as transferred by gift . . .* [etc.].

As you may sense as we go along, many of the features of Section 1022 have their origin in Section 1015 (basis of gifts).

Meaning of "Adjusted Basis"

Subparagraph (A) of subsection 1022(a)(2) expressly reads—

*the **adjusted basis** of the decedent* ['s property].

Said term was first defined in the **1954** Tax Code. It was codified as Section 1011: ***Adjusted Basis for Determining Gain or Loss***. These plain language words alone tell you that one's adjusted basis in property is the benchmark reference for determining (capital) gains or (capital) losses, when conveying legal title to property. The conveyance transaction may be by sale, exchange, gift, inheritance, or other disposition of the property.

In more formal language, Section 1011(a): ***General Rule***, is:

*The adjusted basis for determining the gain or loss from the sale or **other disposition of property**, whenever acquired, shall be the basis (determined under **section 1012** or other applicable sections of this subchapter) and subchapters C (relating to corporate distributions and adjustments), K (relating to partners and partnerships), and P (relating to capital gains and losses)), adjusted as provided in **section 1016**.* [Emphasis added.]

Note the cross references to Sections 1012 and 1016. Section 1012 is titled: ***Basis of Property—Cost***; Section 1016 is titled ***Adjustments to Basis***. Section 1012 addresses the basis of property when it is purchased. Most property items are acquired by purchase, rather than by exchange, gift, inheritance, etc. Section 1016 enumerates approximately 30 different kinds of adjustments to basis, regardless of how the property is acquired. The longer property is held, the more adjustments there are.

To give you a down-to-earth visual feel of what Section 1011 is all about, we present Figure 5.1. Our purpose in doing so is to give you adequate notice of what basis records are expected of you before your demise, or of your executor after your demise.

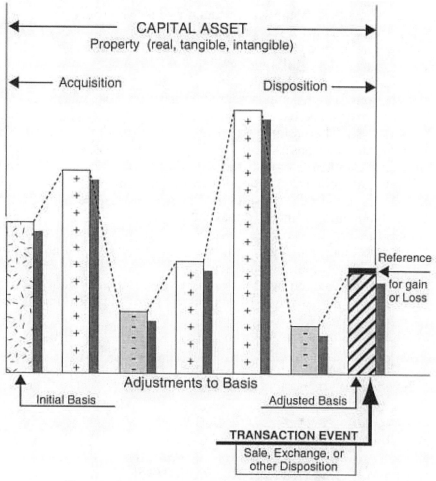

Fig. 5.1 - Conceptual Changes in Tax Basis Over Time

Let us illustrate with a simple example of the need for attention to basis accounting. Suppose you bought 100 shares of stock in a mutual fund. You paid $15 per share at the time (total investment $1,500). You hold the shares for five years, after which you sell them. During the 5-year holding period, you were paid taxable dividends, nontaxable dividends, stock dividends, and stock splits. You let all the dividends and distributions, including capital gain distributions, roll over. You now have 135 shares of stock. What is your basis, as adjusted, in each of your shares?

You have a problem with this, don't you? Most everyone does. This is because only a few persons keep a running account of their basis adjustments as they occur. We want you, as an estate planner and organizer to be different.

The rollover of taxable dividends and taxable capital gain distributions is a plus adjustment to basis. You have added capital to your investment because, separately, you'll be paying tax on these items. The assignment of nontaxable dividends and other property distributions is a minus adjustment to basis. Nontaxable dividends and property distributions constitute the return of some of your own money. If you allow these to roll over, there is no change in your basis. A stock dividend increases the number of shares you hold, with no outlay of money on your part. This dilutes the basis in each of your initially acquired shares. A stock split also increases your number of shares without your contributing any additional money.

Are you beginning to see what we mean about basis adjustments? Or, as statutorily expressed: "Adjustments to basis"?

A $1,300,000 Step-Up Allowed

The fundamental thrust of Section 1022 is its general rule, subsection (a). Its paragraph (2) reads—

*The basis of the person acquiring property from a decedent [after 2009] **shall be the lesser of**—*

(A)   the adjusted basis of the decedent, or

(B)   the fair market value of the property at the date of the decedent's death

In other words, if a decedent's adjusted basis in his gross estate were $1,000,000 (say) and its FMV were $5,000,000 (say), an inheritor's initial basis in that property would be $1,000,000. Since no money changed hands, the transfer is like a gift.

Be introduced now to subsection (b): ***Basis Increase for Certain Property***. "Basis increase." Isn't this the same as step-up in basis? Of course it is. We view this as a trace of wisdom when abruptly shifting from the FMV basis rule to the adjusted basis rule. It softens the tectonic strain just a bit.

How much step-up in basis is allowed?

Answer: Subsection (b)(2)(B) states quite clearly that—

*In the case of **any estate, the aggregate basis increase*** [shall be] *$1,300,000.* [Emphasis added.]

We have no idea where the $1,300,000 amount came from. No rationale is given in the Committee Reports on P.L. 107-16. It is an attempt, we believe, to preserve some of the vestiges of the step-up to FMV basis, which decedents before 2010 have enjoyed.

Thus, in the simple example above, the $1,000,000 adjusted basis estate could have a carryover basis up to $2,300,000 (1,000,000 + 1,300,000). That's in the aggregate (sum total).

If there were multiple properties in the decedent's gross estate, as would be most likely, the prescribed $1,300,000 basis increase has to be allocated property-by-property. No one preferred asset for step-up can be favored. Computationally, this presents a dilemma. It deprives the executor of any discretion in the basis increase. As depicted in Figure 5.2, is the allocation based on the total adjusted basis of the estate or on the FMV of the gross estate?

The tax law on point, subsection 1022(b)(2)(A), does not say. It says only that—

The basis increase . . . for any property is the portion of the aggregate basis increase that is allocated to the property.

Ordinarily, one allocates property to an inheritee based on its FMV: not on its adjusted basis. Therefore, without any regulatory guidance to the contrary, our surmise is that gross estate FMV will be the allocating yardstick. Let us illustrate.

Consider that there is a $100,000 carryover basis asset, the FMV of which is $500,000 in a gross estate of $2,000,000. Its allocated portion of the gross estate would be:

[1] $500,000 ÷ 2,000,000 = 0.25 or 25%

The allocable basis increase would be:

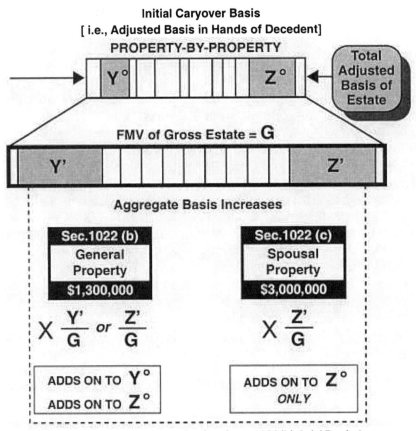

Initial Caryover Basis
[i.e., Adjusted Basis in Hands of Decedent]

Fig. 5.2 - The Allocation Principle for Sections 1022(b) & (c)Basis Increases

[2] $1,300,000 x 0.25 = $325,000

After which the modified (partially stepped-up) carryover basis would be [1] plus [2], namely:

[3] $100,000 + $325,000 = $425,000.

All of this means that for post-2009 estate organization purposes, you have to plan quite differently. In addition to inventorying and FMVing every significant (marketable) item of property, you have to establish its allocable basis increase fraction or percentage. This is a different task from what you had thought about before, isn't it?

Loss Property Basis Increase

The amount of $1,300,000 above is designated in the Tax Code as the *Aggregate Basis Increase.* It's the general increase rule. Additionally, certain specific increases in adjusted basis are allowed for: (1) capital loss carryovers, (2) net operating loss carryovers, and (3) casualty and theft losses. Official authorization for these basis increases is prescribed by subparagraph (C) of subsection 1022(b)(2): *Limit Increased by Unused Built-in Losses and Loss Carryovers.* We cite subparagraph (C) in full, as follows:

The limitation under subparagraph (B) [the $1,300,000] shall be increased by—

(I)   the sum of the amount of any capital loss carryover under Section 1212(b), and the amount of any net operating loss carryover under Section 172, which would (but for the decedent's death) be carried from the decedent's last taxable year to a later taxable year of the decedent, plus

(ii)   the sum of the amount of any losses that would have been allowable under Section 165 if the property acquired from the decedent had been sold at fair market value immediately before the decedent's death.

Under the pre-2010 step-up to FMV basis rule at time of death, the above three specified types of losses would have been self-adjusting or self-eliminating. Except in the case of having a surviving spouse who had filed a joint income tax return (Form 1040) with the decedent, no income allowable losses are carried over after death. This adjusted basis increase rule applicable after 2009 applies the "fairness doctrine" retroactively. This is good.

The retroactive allowance of a basis increase to compensate for otherwise lost tax losses, adds another new dimension to estate organization and planning. Not only must one have good adjusted basis records on his or her property, one must also have (if applicable) good tax loss records as well. In Figure 5.3, we try to portray what some of these loss records might be.

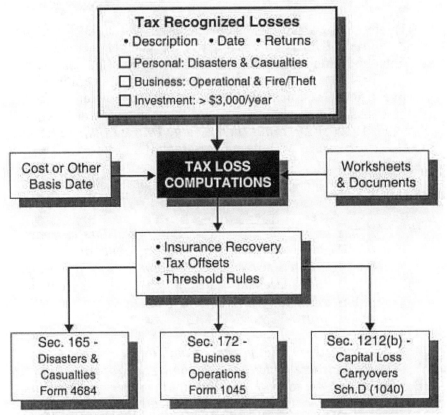

Fig. 5.3 - Income Tax Losses for Decedent's Basis Adjustments

Particularly note in the lower portion of Figure 5.3 that, if tax loss carryovers are applicable to your situation, the following schedules attached to Form 1040 are necessary:

Sched. D   ***Capital Gains and Losses*** [re investment assets]
Form 1045   ***Application for Net Operating Loss Refund*** [re business assets]
Form 4684   ***Casualties and Thefts*** [re personal assets]

Our take on subparagraph (C) is this. All unusable income tax loss carryovers (because of death) are added back dollar-for-dollar. The add-back goes to increase the adjusted basis in each loss item. This makes good capital accounting sense. Suppose, for example, that one purchased a piece of business equipment for $100,000. That's his actual cost basis in it. In transit from the factory to the decedent's predeath place of business, there was a major highway accident. After all insurance and reimbursements, there was a net casualty loss of $35,000 to the equipment. Thus, the decedent owner's adjusted basis in that equipment became $65,000 (100,000 – 35,000). After filing all of the proper tax loss forms, the allowable — but unusable — tax loss might be $25,000.

Disregarding any aggregate basis increase, the loss basis increase would be $25,000. It would not be the $35,000 actual loss in value. Because of "threshold rules" when computing tax losses, a tax allowable loss and one's actual loss in property are not one and the same. That's why the features depicted in Figure 5.2 are so important when claiming loss property basis increases allowed by Section 1022(b)(2)(C).

Spousal Property Basis Increase

In addition to the $1,300,000 general basis increase, there is an up to $3,000,000 spousal property basis increase [Sec. 1022(c)(2)(B). Both the general increase and the spousal increase are *aggregate* increases. This means that both basis increases of targeted property must be apportioned on a fractional or percentage basis. As we tried to depict in Figure 5.2, the numerator of the fraction is the FMV of the targeted property; the denominator is the gross FMV of all property in (or to be in) the decedent's estate.

The sequence of apportioned increases is, first, the general basis increase, followed by the spousal basis increase. The overall effect is that a decedent's total modified carryover basis could be enhanced in inheritee hands by as much as $4,300,000 (1,300,000 + 3,000,000). This is in recognition of basis adjustment realities going back many decades.

For illustration purposes, let us assume that the targeted spousal property has an initial adjusted basis of $150,000. Its FMV is $600,000. The gross FMV of the decedent's estate is

$3,000,000. The fractional increase for apportionment purposes would be 0.20 or 20% [600,000 ÷ 3,000,000]. The general basis increase would be $1,300,000 x 0.20 or $260,000. The spousal basis increase would be $3,000,000 x 0.20 or $600,000. Adding all three of these basis items together, the modified carryover basis in the targeted spousal property would be—

[1] Initial carryover basis: $ 150,000
    PLUS
[2] General basis increase: 260,000
    PLUS
[3] Spousal basis increase: 600,000
    EQUALS $1,010,000

We've already told you that the targeted spousal property FMV is $600,000. Can that item claim a basis increase to $1,010,000 ($410,000 more than its FMV)?

Fair Market Value Limitation

Enter now paragraph (2) of subsection 1022(d): *Definitions and Special Rules*. This paragraph reads in full as—

The adjustments under subsections (b) [general basis increase] *and (c)* [spousal basis increase] *shall not increase the basis of any* [ownership] *interest in property acquired from the decedent above its* [FMV] *in the hands of the decedent as of the date of the decedent's death.*

Thus, in the last illustration above, even though the computationally authorized modified basis would be $1,010,000, its FMV of $600,000 would be limiting. This FMV basis limitation at death is no different from the step up to FMV basis rules in effect prior to 2010. The real difference is that the basis increase rules after 2009 are more complicated and, therefore, more subject to legal controversy than the simplicity of step up.

By controversy, we mean: What happens to the unused computational excess of $41,000 above the FMV limitation above? Is it available for assignment to other spousal property? Maybe so, but we don't really know. These are the kinds of "loose ends" that Congress has not yet addressed.

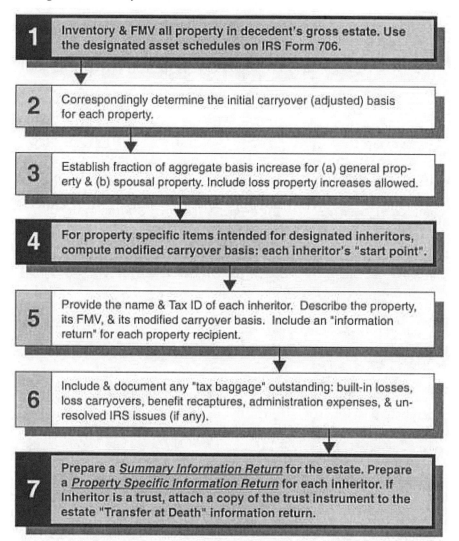

1 Inventory & FMV all property in decedent's gross estate. Use the designated asset schedules on IRS Form 706.

2 Correspondingly determine the initial carryover (adjusted) basis for each property.

3 Establish fraction of aggregate basis increase for (a) general property & (b) spousal property. Include loss property increases allowed.

4 For property specific items intended for designated inheritors, compute modified carryover basis: each inheritor's "start point".

5 Provide the name & Tax ID of each inheritor. Describe the property, its FMV, & its modified carryover basis. Include an "information return" for each property recipient.

6 Include & document any "tax baggage" outstanding: built-in losses, loss carryovers, benefit recaptures, administration expenses, & unresolved IRS issues (if any).

7 Prepare a _Summary Information Return_ for the estate. Prepare a _Property Specific Information Return_ for each inheritor. If inheritor is a trust, attach a copy of the trust instrument to the estate "Transfer at Death" information return.

Fig. 5.4 - Steps for Preparing "Property Specific" Information for Inheritors

We try to portray the gist of much of the above in Figure 5.4. We do this because you should be forewarned of the complexities involved. We also do this because subparagraph (3)(A) of subsection 1022(**d**) says—

The executor shall allocate the adjustments under subsections (b) and (c) on the return required by Section 6018.

Tax Code Section 6018; what's that all about?

New Law Section 6018

There are two versions of Section 6018: new law; old law. The old law which expires after December 31, 2009 is/was titled: ***Estate Tax Returns***. This is/was the domain of IRS Form 706 which has been mentioned several times previously. It is/was a comprehensive *tax return* for property transfers at time of death.

The new law (post 2009) version of Section 6018 is titled: ***Returns Relating to Large Transfers at Death***. Subsection 6018(b)(1) defines a "large transfer" as—

All property (other than cash) acquired from a decedent if the fair market value of such property . . . exceeds the dollar amount applicable under Section 1022(b)(2)(B) (without regard to Section 1022(b)(2)(C)) [re unused built-in losses or loss carryovers].

The cross-reference to Section 1022(b)(2)(B) is the $1,300,000 aggregate basis increase generally allowed. Be aware that there is no cross-reference to Section 1022(c), the $3,000,000 additional basis increase for spousal property. Also, be aware that the statutory wording above does **not** refer to the adjusted basis of the decedent. It says: *fair market value* [FMV] *of such property.*

Now we have a thinking threshold of what constitutes a large estate post 2009: an FMV of $1,300,000 (1.3 million).

Furthermore, a large estate may consist of appreciated property that the decedent received by gift within three years of his death. The presumption is that such a gift (or inter vivos transfer) was for less than full and adequate consideration in money or money's worth [Sec. 1022(d)(1)(C)].

The general rule for new law Section 6018, subsection (a) says that if this section applies—

The executor of the estate of a decedent shall make a return containing the information specified in subsection (c) with respect to such property.

The "information specified" is—

(1) the name and Tax ID of the recipient of such property,
(2) an accurate description of such property,
(3) the adjusted basis of such property in the hands of the decedent and its FMV at time of death,
(4) the decedent's holding period for such property,
(5) sufficient information to determine whether any gain on the sale of the property would be treated as ordinary income (instead of capital gain income),
(6) the amount of basis increase allocated to the property under subsection (b) or (c) of Section 1022, **and**
(7) such other information as the IRS may (someday) by regulations prescribe.

Hence, we conclude that, instead of the old law estate *tax* return, the new law requires an INFORMATION RETURN. It is quite conceivable, therefore, that the old IRS Form 706 could be revised into a new Form 706 as an information-at-death return. We offer some thoughts on this in Chapter 6: Post 2009 Thinking.

Gift Tax Repeal in 2010

There are two Sections 6019: *Gift Tax Returns*, old and new. Old Section 6019 expires on December 31, 2009; new Section 6019 expires on December 31, 2010. This is a one year transitional gap between termination of the estate tax and termination of the gift tax. The obvious question arises: What happens if a person dies in 2010?

Answer: that person's executor files a gift tax return. This is because subsection 1022(a)(1), cited previously on page 4-10, treats transfers at death after year 2009 as transfers by gift. Hence, the application of new Section 6019: Gift Tax Returns.

New Section 6019 consists of 140 words. Its subsection (a): *In General*, reads in principal part as—

> *Any individual who in any calendar year makes any transfer by gift . . . shall make a return for such year with respect to the gift tax imposed* [by Sections 2501 through 2505].

The term *any individual* applies to the executor of a decedent dying in year 2010. Similarly, the term *any transfer* applies to transfers at death which are "treated" as transfers by gift. Beginning in 2011, the gift tax is repealed. Also beginning in 2011 a gift information return is required for living persons who make gratuitous gifts (for less than full and adequate consideration).

Gift information returns are directed by new subsection 6019(b): *Statements to be Furnished to Certain Persons*. The statutory essence of this new subsection is—

> *Every person required to make a return under subsection* [6019]*(a) shall furnish to each person whose name is required to be set forth in such return . . . a written statement showing*—
>
> *(2) the information specified in such return with respect to property received by the person* [designated] *to receive* [it].

While gift *tax* returns themselves will be terminated on December 31, 2010, some revision towards gift *information* returns should be anticipated for years 2011 and beyond. It is unthinkable that the IRS would allow millions of dollars in money and property to be gifted to family members without some kind of carryover basis reporting to the IRS and to each property recipient. Until year 2011, full blown gift tax returns (**Forms 709**) will be required. We address these returns quite fully in Chapter 11: Filing Gift Tax Returns.

6

POST 2009 THINKING

Instead Of Step-Up To Fair Market Value Of Property When Acquired From A Decedent, Each Recipient Of Such Property Will Be Informed Of Its Adjusted Carryover Basis. New And/Or Revised Tax Forms Will Be Required. Where No Or Poor Basis Records Are Kept, The IRS Will Be Notified. Since CASH Itself Is Basis, It Could Become The "Property Of Preference" For Some Inheritors. Prior Property Transfers By The Decedent For Insufficient Consideration Will Be More Scrutinized Than In The Past. The Legislative Carrot Being Offered Is Terminating The Estate Tax Rate Of 45% And Replacing It With A 15% Capital Gains Rate.

Have you digested the tax significance of what we have conveyed to you in Chapters 4 and 5? If so, do you recognize that a tectonic shift in federal tax policy is taking place?

The "shift" is from the taxing of gratuitous (no money or service) transfers of property at death, to income taxing the very same property when it is subsequently sold or exchanged by an inheritor. That is, the former estate and GST (generation-skipping transfer) taxation process is (or will be) replaced by an income taxation process. There's no complete elimination of the death tax: there's just a change in its tax characterization.

Assuming that Section 1022 (basis carryover of decedent's property after 2009) continues as presently written, a whole new estate and tax thinking process unfolds. Instead of the executor for the estate paying tax, the burden is shifted to the inheritor recipient. At time of death, the inheritor receives an *Information Return* which identifies the property, designates its carryover basis, then leaves it up to the inheritor to tax dispose of the property as he, she, or it (a trust) sees fit. It could be that the total tax burden may well be less than if the executor paid all of the tax at death. This is certainly what the sponsors of Section 1022 had in mind.

In Figure 6.1, we try to portray this post-2009 shift in tax policy. Such is our focus in this entire chapter. We want to think ahead and try to anticipate what tasks to perform when organizing your own estate and perhaps assisting other members of your family.

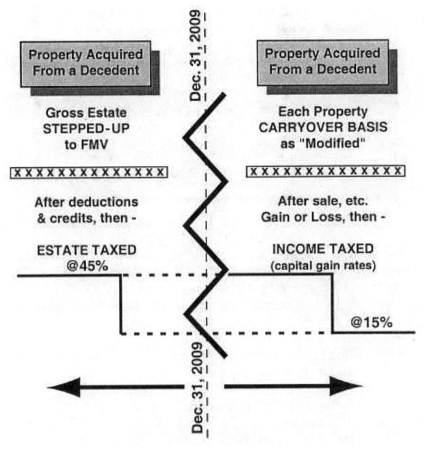

Fig. 6.1 - Shift in Tax Policy When Terminating the Estate Tax

Like a "Pass-Through" Entity

Actually, the tectonic shift portrayed in Figure 6.1 may not be as drastic as you fear. If you've had any experience as a participant in a business partnership, LLC (limited liability company), or S-corporation, you may find the shift to be more understandable and palatable. You may find similarly if you've been a beneficiary of a trust (family, pension, insurance, etc.). All of these arrangements are tax described as: *pass-through* entities. That is, the entity itself pays no tax. The applicable items subject to tax are passed through, proportionally, to entity members who are then taxed. The effect is a dilution of what might have been the entity tax due to differences in income tax rates among individual members filing Forms 1040.

How is the passing-through done?

Answer: By what are commonly known as Schedules K and Schedules K-1. Schedule K is the entity's accounting breakdown of taxable and nontaxable items. Schedule K-1 is a *per recipient* allocation of each corresponding amount on Schedule K. The allocation is based on each recipient's ownership and beneficial interest in the entity. A copy of each Schedule K-1 goes to the IRS and a copy to each entity participant. The general pass-through process is schematized in Figure 6.2.

To enhance your comfort level with our Figure 6.2 depiction, we tell you that there are existing IRS Schedules K and K-1. Said schedules attach to Forms 1065, 1120S, and 1041 as follows:

Form 1065: Partnerships and LLCs

Sched. K   — Partners' (plural) Distributive Share Items
Sched. K-1 — Partner's (singular) Share of Income, Deductions, Credits, etc.

Form 1120S: S Corporations

Sched. K   — Shareholders' (plural) Share of Income, Deductions, Credits, etc.

Sched. K-1 — Shareholder's (singular) Share of Income, Deductions, Credits, etc.

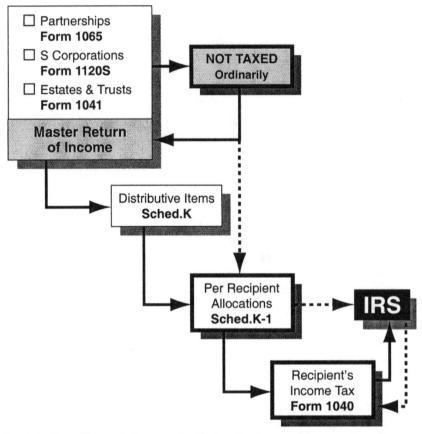

Fig. 6.2 - Pass-Through Concept for Taxing Recipents of Income from Property

Form 1041: Estates and Trusts

No Schedule K currently
Sched. K-1 — Beneficiary's (singular) Share of Income, Deductions, Credits, and *Other Items* (such as distributions of property and capital)

Could the fact that there's no Schedule K to Form 1041 and that its K-1 includes the term "Other items" have any significance? Could it be that some IRS forms designer may be thinking beyond year 2009 . . . and also beyond 2010?

Nevertheless, it is conceivable that a revised Form 706: Basis Carryover of Property Acquired from a Decedent, could evolve. If so, there could be required a Schedule K: Transfer Basis of Each Item in Decedent's Gross Estate, and a Schedule K-1: Inheritor's (singular) Transfer Basis. This is all speculation on our part, of course. But we do sense some "blending" of the current Form 706 with the current Form 1041. We'll try to lay the groundwork for this blending as we go along.

> ***Editorial Note***: Because no IRS Regulations on post-2009 (transfers at death) and post-2010 (transfers by gift) currently exist, some speculation is constructive. There could be a carryover basis Form 707 (at death) and a Form 708 (by gift). These form numbers (707 and 708) are currently unassigned.

Comparing Maximum Tax Rates

It is instructive, momentarily, to compare the maximum tax rates for individual income taxes, estate death taxes, GST transfer taxes, trust income taxes, and capital gain taxes. Certain irresistible trends in federal tax policy appear to be shaping up. If sustained long term by Congress, the trend (towards lower maximum rates) will definitely affect estate organizational efforts.

For year 2006 (and onward, we suspect), individual income tax rates range from a low of 10% to a high of 35% for taxable incomes over $350,000 (350 thousand). Contrast this rate range with 20% to 45% for taxable estates in excess of $2,000,000 (2 million). A footnote to the estate tax rate schedule reads:

*Maximum rates. 2006: 46%; 2007-2009: 45%; **2010**: 35%*

This official footnote signals that Congress clearly intends to limit all estate-type property transfers to 35% no matter how the transfer is characterized in 2010 and thereafter.

Let's switch to Form 1041 for a moment. Said form is officially titled: ***U.S. Income Tax Return for Estates and Trusts***. Its rates range from a low of 15% to a high of 35% for taxable incomes over $10,000. This higher tax rate for a lower income (in the estate or trust) is intentional. It is to discourage retaining income in a trust, and to encourage its pass-through to individual beneficiaries where the tax on $10,000 would be at a 10% rate. Here you have the genesis of the blending of the pass-through and a decedent's basis carryover concepts. It gets better, when we bring in capital gains rates.

Currently, the capital gains rates are **5%** (for incomes under about $50,000), **15%** (the predominate rate for ordinary dispositions of property), **25%** (for depreciation recapture of certain business property), and **28%** (for the disposition of "collectibles": gold coins, gun collections, fine art, antiques, etc.). It's that 15% rate that grabs attention for those owning estate property. A simple numerical illustration will make our point.

Suppose an inheritor (via Schedule K-1) were to receive a taxable amount of $100,000. If this amount were retained by the trust, the tax would be $35,000 ($100,000 x 35%). If passed through to an individual, the tax would be about $25,000, depending on the recipient's personal exemptions, deductions, and credits. But if a capital asset were passed through, with an FMV over basis equal to $100,000, the capital gains tax would be $15,000 ($100,000 x 15%).

Now, let's up the transfer taxable amount to $100,000,000 (100 million). The difference in *virtual* estate tax would be:

Before 2010: $100,000,000 x 35% = $35,000,000 (35 million)
After 2009: $100,000,000 x 15% = $15,000,000 (15 million)

That's a difference of $20,000,000 (20 million) LESS TAX. Obviously, the wealth dynasties will come out ahead, even though the same reduced tax rates will apply to all taxpayers.

Do you now grasp what is really behind the tectonic shift in federal tax policy?

What About Cash Transfers?

Another instructional phenomenon pops out of Section 1022 after year 2009. Its subsection (d)(3)(A) addresses: *Allocation Rules* for basis increases in a decedent's property. Said subsection also cross-references another new tax code section, namely: Section 6018: *Returns Relating to Large Transfers at Death*. Do note that this official title does not characterize the section as a **tax** return. However, its subsection (c): ***Information Required to be Furnished***, clearly implies that Section 6018 is intended to be an **information** return. Could it be Form 707?

There's a particular 3-word clause in Section 6018 that can be easily missed when reading it the first, second, or even third time. That clause within its context is—

This section [6018] *shall apply to all property (**other than cash**) acquired from a decedent if the* [FMV] *of such property exceeds . . .* [$1,300,000]. [Emphasis added.]

Note the emphasized phrase: *Other than cash.* Do you realize what this means? It bodes well for your estate planning while thinkingly alive.

Suppose, now, instead of conveying property to an inheritor after death, it is sold from your estate while alive, and you pay the 15% capital gains tax on it. After the tax is paid, you give the net cash proceeds to any member of your family you choose. Is there any other tax for doing so after 2009?

Answer: No.

Why not?

Answer: There's no carryover basis whatsoever. The cash is after-tax money. As such, it has no initial adjusted basis, no basis increase, and no yardstick for determining capital gain or capital loss. It is a pure pass-through of capital in cash form.

The principle holds true whether the amount of cash is $10,000 (10 thousand); $100,000 (100 thousand); or $1,000,000 (1 million). You can either do this on your own before death, or, at death. You can direct your executor to do it for you (within nine months thereafter). Within nine months after death is the traditional prescribed time for filing IRS Form 706. Have you thought about this type of estate strategy before? Transferring cash instead of property? There could be a substantial reduction in paper work.

"Small Transfer" Interpreted

Let's probe a little further into the introductory wording of Section 6018: ***Returns Relating to Large Transfers at Death***. Its subsection (a), general rule, reads—

If this section applies to property acquired from a decedent, the executor of the estate of such decedent shall make a return containing the information specified [below] *with respect to such property.*

Then immediately following is paragraph (1) of subsection (b): ***Large Transfers***. In succinct part, its wording is—

If the fair market value of such property acquired from the decedent exceeds the dollar amount [$1,300,000] *applicable under section 1022(b)(2)(B) . . . .*

Recall from Chapter 5 that the $1,300,000 (1.3 million) amount is the general property increase in basis allowed by subsection 1022(b)(2)(B). Thus, our interpretation is that no matter what a decedent's initial basis carryover of his property may be, all or a portion of it may be stepped-up (increased) to $1,300,000. This seems to be what is intended, so long as the total of all such actual FMVs does not exceed $1,300,000. The implication is that any gross estate FMV greater than $1,300,000 would be considered a "large estate" . . . or more correctly, a *large transfer* (the Section 6018 title words). Therefore, conversely, any property amount totaling $1,300,000 in FMV or less must be a "small transfer." Would this not be so?

It follows from the above that a small transfer amount could be carved from a large estate and be isolated unto itself. We take this position regardless of the FMV dollar size of one's estate. All property of a decedent, regardless of all else, must be inventoried and FMVed. We portray this carve out concept and its results in Figure 6.3. There is no escape from FMVing.

Suppose a gross estate FMVed at $7,000,000. It consisted of 25 separately identifiable property items, say. If 10 of the property FMV totaled $1,300,000 (or nearly so), why not simply set those items aside. Disregard any basis carryovers and any basis increase allocations. Think of this $1,300,000 of property set asides as your *tax exempt estate*. It would be if sold immediately or shortly after death. Because the decedent's basis carryover would be its FMV, there would be no capital gains tax to pay!

Think about this for a moment.

If your gross estate were \$1,300,000 or less, FMVing is all your executor would need to do. If more than \$1,300,000 — say, the \$7,000,000 amount above — you would have a two part estate: a small transfer estate and a large transfer estate. The large transfer estate would be \$5,700,000 (7,000,000 – 1,300,000). You need focus on basis carryover accounting only for large transfers. Basis carryover accounting, we believe, will be the bane (source of persistent annoyance) of every executor after 2009. Taxpayers, notoriously, are poor basis records keepers.

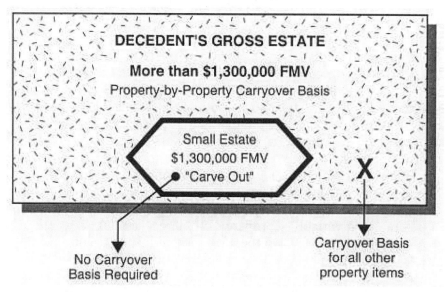

Fig. 6.3 - Separation of "Small Estate" from Larger Estate over \$1,300,000

If No Basis Records

Section 6018: ***Large Transfers at Death***, anticipates that there may be poor or no basis records kept by the decedent. Regardless, the executor's primary responsibility is to inventory, describe, and FMV all property in a decedent's estate. This he/she must do to establish the gross estate. Doing so is independent of whether or not basis records are available. Then the executor must make a conscientious effort to determine: *the adjusted basis of such property in the hands of the decedent* [Sec. 6018(c)(3)]. What happens if no reliable basis records can be found?

Enter, now, paragraph (4) of subsection (b) of Section 6018. Said paragraph is titled: ***Returns by Trustees or Beneficiaries***. Said paragraph reads in full as:

*If the executor is unable to make a complete [information] return as to any property acquired from or passing from the decedent, the executor [then] shall include in the return a description of such property and the name of every person holding a **legal or beneficial interest** therein. Upon notice from the [IRS], such person **shall in like manner** make a return as to such property.* [Emphasis added.]

This citation makes it mandatory that, if the executor cannot find or reconstruct adequate basis records, he is legislatively authorized to shift the task to others. Such persons may be trustees (plural) and/or beneficiaries (also plural). No one "other person" need be singled out. When attempting to pin the basis burden on any of many persons, watch out for fireworks and finger pointing. This reinforces our conviction that for large estate transfers, tax basis matters dominate. This is a direct consequence of repealing the former estate and GST taxation processes. No basis carryovers were required before 2010: just FMVs.

Almost invariably, property in large estates (exceeding $1,300,000 in value) is imbedded in multiple and interlocking trusts of one form or another. Tracing the legal and beneficial interests therein is no easy task. Often, probate proceedings are required to clarify matters. Probate proceedings in state courts are always contentious, time consuming, and costly. Protecting the executor from possible dead-end delays, reflects the wisdom of Section 6018(b)(4) above.

Accordingly, we anticipate that IRS Form 706 revised for year 2010 and thereafter will include such informational queries as:

- *Has the adjusted basis been established for all property included in this return?*   ☐ *Yes,*   ☐ *No.*

- *If "No", identify such property by item number and schedule herein.* ▶_____

- *If "No," give names, identification numbers, and addresses of those persons or entities **to be contacted by IRS**.*

Trustees ▶_____

Beneficiaries ▶_____

When a trustee or beneficiary is contacted by the IRS for tax basis information, anticipate a wild ride of testiness and evasiveness. As a large estate owner, provide the most complete property basis information that you can to your executor. Then instruct him or her to stand firm against inevitable legal attacks. To counter such challenges, you must provide your executor with ample resources in cash.

Property Owned by Decedent

Because of basis carryover rules after 2009, one must expect legal testiness therewith. Attorneys for trustees and for beneficiaries will open up a whole Pandora's box of probate and tax issues. This is because large transfers of property interests wind their way back through many years of property acquisitions, and transit many hands, causing basis records to get jumbled and misplaced. This is particularly true for real estate holdings, publicly-traded securities, closely-held business interests, gratuitous family trusts, and life insurance and annuity contracts.

To address such basis and ownership concerns (it is the owner who can be compelled to provide records), Section 1022 includes a paragraph labeled: ***Rules Relating to Ownership*** [Sec. 1022(d)(1)(B). This is a 560-word tax law. The idea behind such rules is that tax basis carryover issues arise only if property was owned by the decedent at the time it was transfer-designated to others. One cannot bequeath property to his heirs or to others if he does not own it. Rather than citing the rules verbatim, we'll paraphrase them. There are four such rules that are pertinent.

Rule [1] *Jointly held property.* Property owned by the decedent and another person as joint tenants with right of survivorship or tenants by the entirety shall be treated as—

(i)   owned 50% by the decedent if the only other person is the surviving spouse,

(ii)   owned by the decedent to the proportionate extent of consideration paid by the decedent upon its acquisition, and

(iii)   owned by the decedent to the extent of its value divided by the number of joint tenants involved.

Rule [2] *Revocable trusts.* Property transferred into revocable trust by the decedent during his lifetime, shall be treated as owned by the decedent at his death.

Rule [3] *Powers of appointment.* The decedent shall not be treated as owning any property by reason of holding a power of appointment with respect to such property.

Rule [4] *Community property.* Without regard to carryover basis rules, community property between decedent and spouse shall be treated as owned by, and acquired from, the decedent if at least one-half of the whole of such property is treated as owned by the decedent.

Except for property owned by a decedent and spouse, clarifying the separate ownership interest of each co-tenant (for carryover basis purposes) can be tricky and controversial. There are so many financial factors and horse-trades involved. You start with "Day 1" when the property was initially acquired. Then you diligently pin down, in dollars or dollar equivalents, each co-owner's contribution of capital to the co-owned property.

Insufficient Consideration Transfers

To establish full ownership of property, one must produce documentation that he or she did one of the following: purchased it, acquired it by exchange, acquired it by gift, or inherited it. Here, the term "documentation" means that which is prepared responsibly by someone other than by the property-owner claimant. Self-created records — even via computer sophistication — are not credible documentation in IRS eyes.

On this point, IRS Regulation § 1.1014-4(c): *Records; adjustment to basis*, states that the owner of property—

Shall maintain records showing in detail all [costs paid or services rendered], *deductions, distributions, or other items for which adjustment to basis is required . . . and shall furnish to the* [IRS] *with respect to those adjustments as* [it] *may require.*

The bracketed clause: [costs paid or services rendered] is author included as a substitute cross reference to Regulation § 20.2043-1: *Transfers for insufficient consideration.* Said regulation is due to sunset after year 2009 and be recast as a revised regulation under Section 1022. The term: *Insufficient consideration*, reflects the fact that no bona fide sale took place at which adequate and full consideration in money and money's worth (in property or services) was paid. If the price paid was less than its full FMV, any transfer of property therewith is treated as a gift. In Figure 6.4 we depict why the IRS is so concerned about gratuitous transfers of property for inadequate consideration.

For example, suppose the decedent before his death acquired property FMV worth $100,000 from his brother. The decedent paid $15,000 for it. The brother was in a high income tax bracket and had a large estate of his own. The brother could well afford to look the other way with regard to the $85,000 (100,000 – 15,000) insufficiency. The executor finds a hand written note by the brother that $100,000 was paid. The executor also finds a $15,000 canceled check. What does Section 1022 say about this kind of transfer of property?

Said transfers are addressed by subsection 1022(d)(1)(C): *Property acquired by decedent by gift* [or for insufficient consideration] *within 3 years of death.* Subparagraph (i) of this subsection says—

Subsections (b) and (c) [of Section 1022 re allowable basis increases] *shall not apply to property acquired by the decedent by gift or by inter vivos transfer* [between living persons] *for less than adequate and full consideration in money or money's worth during the 3-year period ending on the date of the decedent's death.*

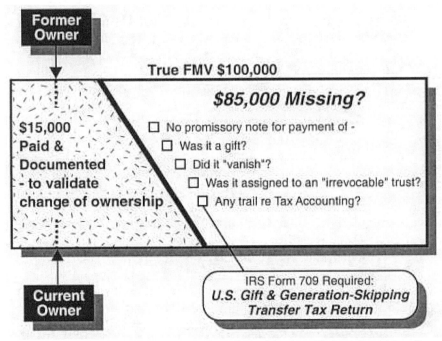

Fig. 6.4 - Concern When Property Transferred for Insufficient Consideration

Translation: If the decedent can document that he paid $15,000 for property FMV worth $100,000, his initial (and only) carryover basis for that property would be $15,000. This is so whether before or within three years of his death. If the property was acquired within three years of death, no general or spousal basis increases would be allowed. Correspondingly, the disallowance of any basis increase clearly implies that, if the $15,000 "consideration" could not be documented, there would be no carryover basis for that property whatsoever.

Property Acquired from Decedent

Subsection 1022(e) addresses the issue of property acquired from a decedent which may or may not have been itemized in his gross estate. Such addressment is required because all property acquired from a decedent, whether before or after his death, and whether or not in the decedent's hands at time of death, has to be assigned a carryover basis. This is a legislative mandate. Its purpose is to *tax access* all transfers of property that may have escaped taxation in the past.

The statutory wording of subsection (e): **Property Acquired from the Decedent**, reads primarily as—

The following property shall be considered to have been acquired from the decedent:

(1)   Property acquired by bequest, devise, or inheritance, or by the decedent's estate from the decedent.

(2)   Property transferred by the decedent during his lifetime—
   (A)   to a qualified revocable trust, or
   (B)   to any other trust with respect to which the decedent reserved the right to make any change in the enjoyment thereof through the exercise of a power to alter, amend, or terminate the trust.

*(3)   Any other property passing from the decedent by reason of death to the extent that such property **passed without consideration**.*

Passing property into sophisticated-sounding gratuitous trusts without consideration is an inbred right-of-passage for wealth holders who are brilliant and fearless. They have the money to fight the IRS every step of the way. They claim their arrangements are **Irrevocable Trusts**.   Often, instead, they involve fraudulent transfers. They are fraudulent to the extent that no transfer tax is paid, or that no full and adequate tax accounting has been made. A truly legitimate irrevocable trust requires the filing of IRS Form 709: *U.S. Gift and Generation-Skipping Transfer Tax Return.*

The tone of legislation above and our depiction in Figure 6.5 are all encompassing.   They leave little interpretive slack in property transfers where tax errors and omissions have occurred and where tax avoidance strategies have been employed. The wording is intended to catch up with, and close up, all insufficiently tax disclosed property transfers of the past. This catch-up, close-up treatment holds whether the transfers are by U.S. citizens or U.S. residents within the U.S. or within foreign jurisdictions.

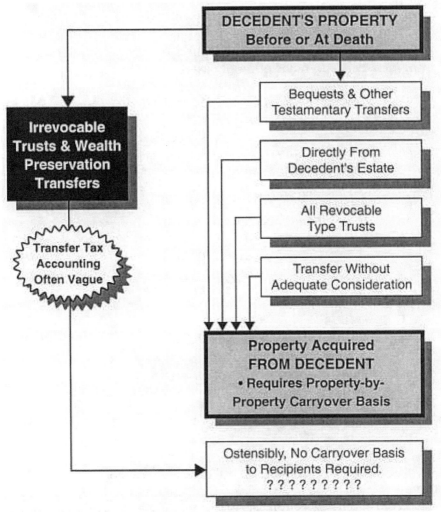

Fig. 6.5 - Role of Revocable vs. Irrevocable Transfers of Decedent's Property

An interesting (and instructional) sidenote to the above pertains to IRD sources. The letters "IRD" stand for: **I**ncome in **R**espect of **D**ecedent (Tax Code Section 691). IRD income is that which was due the decedent before his death, but was not paid until after his death.

IRD income is not treated as "property" because there is no documentable basis in it. Such income passes directly to living heirs of the decedent, where it is income taxed by them. The heirs, on their Form 1040 returns, characterize the IRD income exactly as it would have been income taxed had the decedent received it while alive. The heirs also get a proportionate deduction against the IRD amount for any tax paid on the IRD by the decedent's estate. Most heirs are quite unaware of IRD and its ramifications.

On this point, subsection (f) of Section 1022 says that—

This section [re carryover basis, etc.] ***shall not apply*** *to property which constitutes a right to receive an item of income in respect of a decedent.*

Still, Questions Remain

Subsection (g) of Section 1022: ***Certain Liabilities Disregarded***, raises more questions than it settles. The essence of said subsection is:

In determining whether gain is recognized on the acquisition of property—

> *(A) from a decedent by a decedent's estate, and*
> *(B) from the decedent's estate by any beneficiary,*

and in determining the adjusted basis of such property, liabilities in excess of basis shall be disregarded.

What is subsection (g): Liabilities Disregarded, getting at?

In an indirect way, it is saying that a negative basis (below zero) in inherited property is not tax recognized. If it were recognized, the computed gain would exceed the actual proceeds from the sale. This doesn't make economic sense. Why should one pay capital gains tax on phantom money?

For example, suppose an item of property acquired from a decedent had a negative carryover basis of $100 [indicated as either <100> or –100]. If the item sold for $1,000, say, its capital gain would be $1,100 (1,000 –, – 100 or 1,000 + 100) [a minus, minus is a plus]. The effect would be that of paying capital gains tax on $100 of capital loss money. Doesn't make sense, does it?

Nor does it make sense for the mandated carryover basis rules to disregard previously allowable deductions on Form 706. Such deduction items are/were: (1) funeral expenses, (2) administrative expenses (attorneys, accountants, appraisers), (3) debts and mortgages of the decedent, and (4) other miscellaneous costs. These are itemized on Schedules J, K, and L of Form 706 and are deductible from the gross estate. Post 2009, are these ordinary and necessary expenses — liabilities of the decedent's estate — to be disregarded altogether?

Also, what happens to Schedule M (706): Bequests to Surviving Spouse, Schedule O (706): Bequests to Charity, and property taxes and death taxes paid to foreign governments and to state governments within the U.S.?

Ostensibly, Section 1022(c)(2): *Spousal Property Basis Increase* up to $3,000,000 is a substitution for Schedule M (706). But when you read the 600-word "fine print" for spousal property qualifications, one is left in a quandary. Does the fine print virtually guarantee up to $3,000,000 increase, or does it provide loopholes for wealth dynasties to exceed this amount?

Could it be that all disregarded liabilities could be assigned to IRS **Form 1041**: *U.S. Income Tax Return for Estates and Trusts*? On such form (page 1: mid-portion), there's an INCOME section and, separately, a DEDUCTIONS section. Thus, under post-2009 rules, we believe that a closer coordination between Form 706 (for carryover basis information) and Form 1041 will be required. We blend these two processes as we move forward thinkingly.

7

GOALS TO PURSUE

The Best Evidence Of Your Dedication To Organizing Your Estate Is To Procure In Hand A Copy Of IRS Form 706. Also Include Form 709 And Form 1041. Skimming Through Them (And Their Instructions) Will Trigger Self Thoughts On What To Do And What Not To Do. If Married, Each Spouse Has His AND Her Own Gross Estate. If Not 50/50, Discuss The MARITAL DEDUCTION INCLUSION Rule. Classify Your Net Distributable Estate Into Low-Value And High-Value Assets. Sell The Low Values Within 9 Months After Your Demise Via ESTATE Form 1041. Designate In Percentiles Your Assignments Of Income And Property To Your Heirs.

Very few noteworthy accomplishments are achieved during life without setting goals. Goals are especially important when tackling such a daunting task as: *Organizing Your Estate . . . While Thinkingly Alive*. There are two classes of goals: general and specific. A general goal points you in a *general direction*. Maybe you proceed in that direction without change; maybe you don't. More than likely, you'll redirect your direction as you gain experience along the way. And, still, you may not reach the directional end that you seek. Nevertheless, without some kind of directional goal, you wander, flounder, . . . and procrastinate. Floundering is what happens in most estate affairs. The result, too often, is that organizing one's estate never gets done.

To help you get started, here's an example of the kind of general goal that you might set. Say to yourself:

"Before senile dementia takes over my life, I want my gross estate formulated in such a way that—

(a)   Its transfer to my heirs is a "no brainer" for *my* designated executor;

(b)   IRS Form 706 must be prepared, filed, and all related debts and taxes paid within *9 months* of my demise . . . with no extensions; and

(c)   My estate, except for my personal residence and other designated high-value assets, shall be in *liquid form* or readily convertible thereto."

In contrast to such a general goal as above, certain *specific goals* need to be formulated. Because of the time frame of this book, any specific goals chosen must be a blend of near-term objectives (before 2010) and those beyond 2009. In either case, your objective should be to inventory, appraise, rearrange, and reformulate selected categorical assets for simplicity of identity, valuation, and basis transfer. Most of the subsequent chapters hereto focus on specific goals.

In this chapter, we want to focus on those general estate-simplifying goals which we think are laudable . . . and achievable. If you concur, what we present can be regarded as a self-guiding roadmap. Use the portions of it that appeal to you. If there are portions on which you want further guidance, please wait until after you've read any relevant chapters which follow. Then you may want specific professional guidance. We caution you, however, to keep professionals at bay as long as you possibly can. Take the time necessary to glean knowledge first-hand.

Get Forms 706, 709, & 1041 Now

Here's a little test of your resolve to organize your estate while you can. It will cost you nothing other than search time on the IRS's web site: **www.irs.gov** and/or a phone call to the IRS's Forms center: **1-800-829-3676**. We want you to physically get into your hands a copy of Form 706 and its instructions, a copy of Form 709 and its instructions, and a copy of Form 1041 and its instructions. Form 706 is 40 pages long and has 30 pages of instructions; Form 709 is 4 pages long and has 12 pages of instructions; and Form 1041 is 10 pages long and has 12 pages of instructions: Total 142 pages in all. You may find it impractical to download this number of pages from your computer; that's why we give the IRS Forms phone number above. If you phone, allow about 10 days for delivery by mail.   ·

The correct full title of each of the above three forms is:

Form 706:   *United States Estate (and Generation-Skipping Transfer) Tax Return.*

Form 709:   *United States Gift (and Generation-Skipping Transfer) Tax Return.*

Form 1041: *U.S. Income Tax Return for Estates and Trusts.*

Don't worry. We do not expect you to fill out any of these forms. We just want you to have them in your hands. Then, we suggest you leaf through each form and its instructions, page by page, glancing at the headings and subheadings. We want you to appreciate more fully what your successors will have to do on your behalf. You've probably never seen, or held any of these forms before. This is your chance to one-upmanship those professionals who will take over when you are gone.

By your skimming and glancing through Forms 706, 709, and 1041, and their instructions (the tax rate schedules are in the instructions), one of two things will happen. Either you will give up and say to yourself: "Let the professionals handle it when I am gone." Or, you may say to yourself: "Hmm! I think I can simplify things enough so that my executor can take charge. I'd rather my heirs get my money than the professionals."

All that we expect of you is a reasonable determination to change your status quo by earnestly wanting to organize and simplify your estate affairs. If you already have a 35-to-50-page *trust* tome, we ask that you review it to see if it assists you in any way towards the preparation of any of the listed IRS forms.

Prepare Your Executor

No matter what you now do or don't do, Form 706 is the *central highway* through all of your estate affairs. Mandatorily, it starts at date of death and ends upon estate closure, as evidenced by an Acceptance Letter from the IRS. We think it should start sooner than the onset of any senility that may await you. Senility is difficult to self-diagnose, so don't wait too long.

Regardless of the FMV of your gross estate, Form 706 is an excellent starting point for organizational purposes. One of your first tasks therewith is to have in mind who your executor may be. We suggest thinking beyond your spouse, who may survive you. No matter what, you MUST APPOINT your own executor. Don't you dare let the legal system do it for you!

Here's an example on point: true case. The decedent was an unmarried man. He had no children and his two older siblings had predeceased him. He lived alone in a small apartment. Because he didn't answer phone calls for several days, the landlady and a policeman entered the apartment and found him dead. After the coroner took the body away, the landlady called the local bar association to recommend an attorney who would handle small estates. The attorney ascertained the decedent's gross estate to be $262,500 (5 CDs at $50,000 each; $10,000 in checking/savings; and a car and TV worth $2,500). The attorney then petitioned the probate court to have himself appointed as the decedent's "personal representative" and executor.

Some *two years* later, the estate was settled. The unpaid debts amounted to $2,160. The accounting fees were $850; the cleaning and hauling costs were $400; the clerical and filing costs came to $130; the legal costs and fees came to $198,960. Yes: $198,960! These administration costs left exactly $60,000 to be distributed to six nephews and nieces . . . at $10,000 each.

If you have no adult children of your own, surely there would be some member in your family whom you could appoint. The simplest way is to make the appointment in your **own handwriting** (not by typewriter or computer). Date and sign a piece of nonletterhead paper that (in effect) says—

Upon my demise, I hereby appoint the following person or persons as my executor:

_____, *Executor*

_____, *Successor Executor*

or,

_____, *Co-Executor*
_____, *Co-Executor*

A better way is to make your appointment by means of a will, which is witnessed or notarized.

706 Directed at Executor

If you and/or your executor have a Form 706 in hand, you'll note that it is addressed to your executor only. It is *not* addressed to you as a prospective decedent. For example, there is a statement on its page 2 which says (boldly)—

You must attach the death certificate.

Obviously, you can't make such attachment on your own. Either your executor or a professional does it for you.

On page 2 of the Form 706 instructions, the subheading: *Executor*, reads—

The term "executor" means the executor, personal representative, or administrator of the decedent's estate. If none of these is appointed, qualified, and acting in the United States, every person in actual or constructive possession of any property of the decedent is considered an executor and must file [Form 706].

It is worthy to note that, at the bottom of the front page of Form 706, it is your executor who signs the form . . . *Under penalties of perjury.*

In the headportion of Form 706, the following information about your executor is required:

• Name of Executor
• Executor's address (also add phone number)
• Executor's Social Security Number

Just below this executor information block, a statement reads:

If decedent died testate [with will], *check here* ⟶ ☐ *and attach a certified copy of the will.*

Note carefully that this statement does **not** say: "Attach a copy of the trust, if any." It says: THE WILL. Consequently, we insist that, even if you have a trust or other nonwill arrangement, you have a will. Then make sure that your executor knows where your will is, among your personal papers. Better yet, provide your executor with a copy of your will.

Coordinate with Spouse

If you are married, your spouse has an estate in his or her own right. Form 706 is a **per decedent** tax return. It is NOT a joint husband and wife return. The head portion of the form asks only for the decedent's name, the decedent's social security number, the decedent's date of birth, and the decedent's date of death. Should both spouses die simultaneously in a common event, there is one Form 706 for spouse A and an entirely separate Form 706 for spouse B. Do one first, then the other.

Since each spouse has a separate gross estate for Form 706 purposes, you should reach an agreement early on with your spouse as to which portion or items of the gross marital estate belong to each of you. If you have been married only once and are still married, the division of marital property is presumed generally to be 50/50. If you have been divorced and now remarried, the 50/50 division will most likely differ. Particularly so, if you have a prenuptial agreement with your present spouse. Also, the marital property division may be non-50/50 due to gifts and inheritances from parents and relatives. In addition, state law has some bearing on the division of property between spouses.

The trend throughout the U.S. is to allow the spouses to agree between themselves as to their marital division of property. No matter how acquired by each spouse, interspousal gifts are no longer transfer tax accountable. Prior to 1982, gifts to one's spouse in excess of $100,000 were transfer taxed . . . but no more [IRC Sec. 2523(a)]. Rather than leaving these matters to chance, it is recommended that if your division of marital property is non-50/50, you coordinate with your spouse the separation of estate items. You may use Figure 7.1 as a guide in this respect. Date and list each separate itemization, and each spouse sign each other's listing as an acknowledgment thereof.

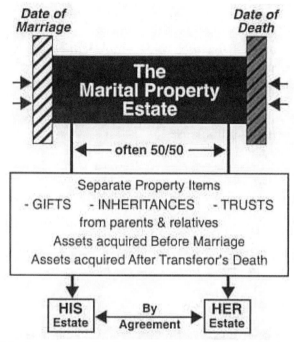

Fig. 7.1 - Agreeing to the Separate Gross Estate of Each Spouse

In durable marriages without major gifts and inheritances from outside the marriage, the acceptance of a 50/50 division is increasingly common. If this is your intention, why not make title matters clear? Have all (or selected) recordable property titled as *Joint Tenancy* . . . with right of survivorship (WROS). The WROS titling does two things, namely: (1) it simplifies the marital division of property for Form 706 purposes at time of death; (2) it avoids probate of said property upon death of the first spouse. In community property states (where everything is 50/50), WROS must be signified. For modest marital estates — less than $3,000,000 — there is really no need for fancy trust arrangements. However, if one's spouse is likely to be incompetent, disabled, or spendthrift, then non-joint tenancy arrangements are preferable.

Discuss the Marital Deduction

Although Form 706 is not a joint spousal return, there is one feature that applies only to a decedent who is married at time of death. The special feature is the marital bequest deduction of Section 2056(a). This section is titled: **Bequests, Etc., to Surviving Spouse; Allowance of Marital Deduction.** With certain exceptions, the marital deduction is virtually unlimited in amount. This one deduction, plus your exemption amount, can totally reduce your pre-2010 transfer tax to zero. But, there's a catch. (Isn't there always?) Thus, you need to discuss this matter appropriately with your spouse.

The substance of Section 2056(a) reads—

*The value of the taxable estate shall, except as limited by subsection (b), be determined **by deducting** from the value of the gross estate an amount equal to the value of any interest which passes or has passed from the decedent to his surviving spouse, but only **to the extent that** such interest **is included** in determining the value of the gross estate.* [Emphasis added.]

In other words, if the marital deduction is claimed, the property value so deducted must derive from one or more of your asset Schedules A through I of Form 706. Said deductible amount must be described and claimed on Schedule M: **Bequests, Etc. to Surviving Spouse.** Schedule M has its own separate instructions. There are technicalities with terminable interests, life estates, qualified trusts, etc. If these technicalities are applicable in your case, and are incomprehensible to you or to your spouse, seek professional counseling thereon. Unfortunately, such counseling may lead to more technicalities and to more incomprehension.

The idea behind the marital deduction allowance is that, while it reduces your Form 706 tax, it increases correspondingly that of your spouse's Form 706. What you deduct, your surviving spouse must include. What is subsequently included, however, may be less than that which you deduct. Between your death and that of your spouse, the element of *consumption* takes place. Indeed, the very reason for the marital deduction is to allow you to provide adequately for your spouse. This is expected of you, should your spouse's portion of the marital gross estate be significantly less than yours, and/or she is much younger than you.

There is still another coordination task that you should review with your spouse . . . and your executor. That is, you should establish some strategic apportionment between the marital deduction and your exemption allowance. The exemption allowance, recall, is $2,000,000 for years 2006, 2007, and 2008; it jumps to $3,500,000 in 2009. It doesn't make sense to reduce your transfer tax to zero (which you could) by the marital deduction alone. If you did, you'd lose the benefit of your exemption allowance. Therefore, you should inform your spouse and instruct your executor to take advantage of *both* the marital deduction *and* your exemption allowance. Obviously, when your Form 706 is prepared you won't be around to strategize on your own. Because so, you must grant your executor sufficient discretionary authority to choose the best arrangement that he can. For some guidance in this regard, Figure 7.2 may be helpful. Be aware, however, that after 2009 the concept presented in Figure 7.2 may no longer be applicable.

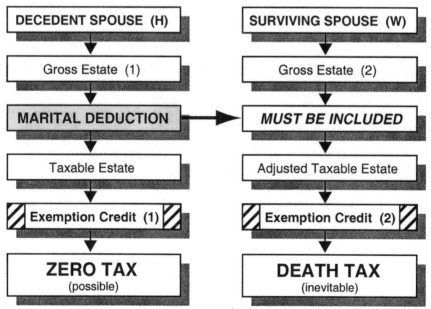

Fig. 7.2 - Effect of Marital Deduction on Surviving Spouse's Estate (pre-2010)

A Word About Form 709

Earlier, along with Form 706, we urged you to get a copy of Form 709 and its instructions. Said form is short-titled: *U.S. Gift & GST Tax Return*. Unless you are already familiar with Form 709, we want you to leaf through it. One reason for this looking and leafing is to convince you that such a form exists and that it has an informational and carryover basis purpose.

While you are alive, you can make gifts to anyone: not just to family. If you die in the year of a gift, coordination between Forms 706 and 709 is required. Until year 2011 (when the gift tax terminates), the gift tax exemption amount is $1,000,000. This means that any gifts you make before 2011 would have to be substantial — at least over $1,000,000 — before any gift tax ultimately applies. You might want to keep the idea in mind that gifts before death could be part of your estate planning. We'll come back to this subject in Chapter 11: Filing Gift Tax Returns (while alive).

The main reason we want to acquaint you with Form 709 is its **transitional role** into post-2009 thinking. To sense this role, you need to take a good look at, and actually read portions of its Schedule A. That schedule's official title is: *Computation of Taxable Gifts (including transfers in trust) (see instructions)*. The instructions for: *Who Must File*, say (in part)—

*You must file a gift tax return (**whether or not any tax is ultimately due**) in the following situations:* [Emphasis added]

- Gifts of more than $12,000 to any one person.
- Certain gifts, called "future interests."
- Split gifts between husband and wife.
- Gifts from a trust, estate, partnership, or corporation.
- If a donor dies before filing a return, the donor's executor must file the return.

Particularly note the emphasized clause: must file . . . *whether or not any tax is ultimately due*. What's the rationale for this mandate? You get part of the answer from the columnar headings in Schedule A (Form 709).

The columnar headings that we want you to read are:

Col. B — • **Donee's** name and address
 • Relationship to donor (if any)
 • Description of gift
 • If gift of securities, give CUSIP number

> *Ed. Note:* CUSIP is Committee on Uniform Security Identification Procedures.

Col. D — *Donor's adjusted basis of gift*
Col. E — Date of gift
Col. F — Valuation at date of gift

Column D: Where (herein) have you seen the term : "adjusted basis" before? Wasn't it in Chapter 5: Carryover Basis Rules? In that chapter, we explained the origin of basis carryover via Code Section 1015: *Basis of Property Acquired by Gifts and Transfers in Trust*. Can you sense now a transitional connection between Form 709 and post-2009 Form 706? It's there, if you visualize the two forms blending into each other.

Example: Reconstruction of Basis

If you make a gift before 2010 or die after 2009, you (or your executor) are faced with the necessity of establishing the adjusted basis of property "in your hands." This can be quite an ordeal. Especially if you acquired and held the property for a long time before its transfer to others. Because of this, we want to illustrate the burden with a true life example.

A young couple, married, had one infant child when they bought their first home. After a few years in the home, it burned down (completely). Although insurance paid for their temporarily renting another home, they had a mortgage to pay on vacant land. After selling the land to pay off the mortgage, they were left with no home . . . and with no money to buy another home.

So, they moved in with the wife's elderly mother. It was a 2 bedroom, 1 bath, 1100 sq. ft. home on 1.75 acres of land. A year later, the mother died and left the home to the couple, who were expecting their second child. The inherited value of the home was $125,000 — its step-up to FMV. Thus, the $125,000 became their initial "acquisition cost."

INHERITED PRINCIPAL RESIDENCE

2 BR/ 1 BATH, 1100 sq.ft. home on 1.75 acres in urban area.

☐ **Appraised FMV when inherited** **$125,000**

Recollections by 4 daughters and 4 sons-in-law:

1.	Addition of 2 new bedrooms	145,000
2.	Replumbing & 2 new bathrooms	32,500
3.	Driveway	9,500
4.	Sprinklers	5,500
5.	Sod & landscape	2,500
6.	Remodeling	35,000
7.	General renovations	20,000
8.	Roof	7,500
9.	French doors	5,400
10.	Patio	20,000
11.	Gravel	2,800
12.	Gazebo	4,000
13.	Storage units (2)	2,400
14.	Walkways (bender boards)	3,500
15.	Heating & air conditioning	5,000
16.	New carpeting	6,700
17.	Greenhouse	7,000
18.	Sewage line (replace septic)	11,000
19.	Other general miscellaneous	30,000
20.	Total refinancing costs (6 times)	50,430

Total Cost of Improvements **402,730**

ADJUSTED BASIS (Day Before Sale) **527,730**

☐ **Property Sold for** **$1,600,000**

Fig. 7.3 - Recollections of Basis Costs Over 30 Yrs. With No Records

Over the next 30 years, they put many improvements in the home, as their family grew and their older children married. They had four daughters and four sons-in-law, each of whom at one time or another moved in with the inheritor couple. By this time, the couple had developed life-threatening lung and throat cancer. Both were heavy (3 packs a day) cigarette smokers. Their cancer treatment costs and other medical expenses necessitated that they sell their home to pay off their debts. At the time of sale, they were terrified over what taxes they'd have to pay, and what the "adjusted basis" in the house sold would be. Over the 30 years of home improvements, they kept no records whatsoever.

Faced with the situation above, how would you proceed?

Since the cancer couple were too sick to help or to remember, their tax preparer called for a *brainstorming session* with their four daughters and their four husbands. All eight had physically participated in the home expansion projects, various renovations, and building code updates (electrical, plumbing, sewerage, etc.). They had vivid recollections of the costs therewith. The results of the brainstorming are presented in Figure 7.3. Subsequently, the reconstructed adjusted basis was accepted by the IRS. It was "accepted" in the sense that the IRS never questioned it.

Our point in Figure 7.3 is this. Even without proper documentation, it is possible to reconstruct a credible adjusted basis in one's property. Lacking all else, brainstorming and best recollections must be reduced to writing BEFORE any basis entry is made on a tax return. Then, if questioned by the IRS, each recollector may offer an affidavit as to his or her knowledge of the facts and circumstances.

Read the "Yes-No" Questions

With regard to IRS questionings on estate matters, Forms 706, 709, and 1041 provide some indicators of what can be asked. For example, on pages 2 and 3 of Form 706, under General Information, there are numerous questions that must be answered "Yes," or answered "No." Leaving any question blank is construed by the IRS as being "Yes." Any "Yes" answer requires that a statement and explanation be attached. The questions are directed to your executor: not to you. Nevertheless, you and your executor should read the questions together, and discuss those items that are relevant. Some of the questions are straightforward; some are tricky; some are highly technical; and some require research and the digging up of old records. We condense these questions for you in Figure 7.4

In some cases, we may have overly condensed the IRS question in Figure 7.4. Question 1 asks about Section 2044 property. What in the world is that?

Estate of:	General Information		
Please check the "yes" or "no" box for each question		Yes	No
1.	Does the gross estate contain any Sec. 2044 property?		
2.	Have Federal gift tax returns ever been filed?		
3.	Was any insurance on the decedent's life not included?		
4.	Did the decedent own any insurance on the life of another?		
5.	Did decedent own any property as a joint tenant with someone other than spouse?		
6.	Did decedent own any interest in a partnership or unincorporated business?		
7.	Did decedent make any transfers described in Sec. 2035, 2036, 2037, or 2038?		
8.	Were any trusts created by decedent during his/her lifetime?		
9.	Did decedent have any power, beneficial interest, or trusteeship in any trust not created by decedent?		
10.	Did decedent ever possess, excercise, or release any general power of appointment?		
11.	Was the marital deduction computed under Public Law 97-34?		
12.	Immediately before death, was decedent receiving an annuity?		

If you answer "yes" to any question, you must attach additional information.

Fig. 7.4 - "Probing Questions" on Form 706: General Information

When you read the official version of Question 1, it refers you to the instructions to Form 706. There in bold caption: *Section 2044 Property*, the instructions read:

Section 2044 property is property for which a QTIP [Qualified Terminable Interest Property] election has been made, or for which a similar gift tax election has been made. For more information, see instructions on the back of Schedule F [Other Miscellaneous Property].

The referenced Schedule F (706) instructions are captioned: ***Decedent Who Was a Surviving Spouse***. The essence of this particular instruction is that—

If the surviving spouse retained his or her interest in the QTIP property at death, the full value of the QTIP property is includible in his or her estate, even though the qualifying income interest terminated at death.

This gets us back to the concept depicted in Figure 7.2. But it also raises a question in our mind re post-2009, when Section 2044 is intended to be terminated.

Apparently, Section 2044 is to be replaced by Section 1022(c): ***Additional Basis Increase for Property Acquired by Surviving Spouse.*** Its paragraph (3) says that—

> *The term "qualified spousal property" [QSP] means:*
> *(A) outright transfer property, and*
> *(B) qualified terminable interest property.*

Thus, the idea of transferring property to one's surviving spouse is retained. However, there's a significant basis difference. Section 2044 permits an unlimited basis step-up to FMV. It could be $10,000,000 or more. In contrast, Section 1022(c)(3) limits the step-up (called: "basis increase") to $3,000,000. Depending on the gross FMV of your estate, the marital deduction feature is something to keep in mind.

In addition to our commentary above, there are numerous other "Yes-No" questions on Form 706, several on Form 709, and nine on Form 1041. We think you should read them all . . . and try to organize your affairs accordingly.

A Word About Form 1041

The **estate** portion of Form 1041: Income Tax Return for Estates and Trusts, should be of prime organizational interest to you. This is because it is prepared by your executor, who has nine months after your death to do those property transfers that you didn't get around to before your senility or demise. You can direct your executor to sell certain property which, compared to your gross estate as a whole, is relatively low in value. In other words, you can direct the immediate sale of all of your low-value assets.

What is a low-value asset?

It is that which is low in value **to the IRS**: not low in value to your heirs (necessarily). With basis carryover rules in mind, it would be any asset that would derive no capital gain when sold. The rationale for justifying Section 1022 (basis carryover) is to make up for lost federal revenue when the estate and GST taxation processes are terminated. Low-value assets are simply not going to provide the IRS with substantial revenue potential that would attract its attention.

Let us give a simple low-value to IRS, yet high-value to your heirs, example. You have $1,000,000 (1 million) FMV in tax-exempt municipal bonds. Your carryover basis in those bonds is $965,000. Muni bonds, characteristically, do not increase or decrease much over time. If the bonds were sold at FMV, there'd be only $35,000 (1,000,000 − 965,000) in capital gains to report to the IRS. At a 15% capital gain rate, that would be only about $5,000 into the U.S. Treasury. This $5,000 represents one-half of one percent on a $1,000,000 asset. If, on the other hand, the bonds FMVed at $965,000 with a basis of $1,000,000 that would be a capital loss of $35,000.

Thus, we think that immediately disposing of low-value assets upon your demise is an ideal way to reduce clutter and uncertainty in your estate. Save the high-value assets for subsequent transfer to heirs and/or to others, either outright or in trust.

Immediate attention to accounting affairs after death is also an opportunity to pass any net losses through to heirs (which can help reduce their own income taxes). Ordinarily, an estate or trust cannot pass losses through to its beneficiaries until the "Final Return" of the estate or trust is filed with the IRS. Unfortunately, attorneys want to "force-blend" trust affairs with estate affairs so that there is no accounting distinction between the two. This means that if your trust doesn't terminate for 20 years, any tax losses that develop within nine months of your demise have to wait 20 years to be passed through.

To pass legitimate losses through promptly, it is imperative that there be two separate EINs (Employer/Entity Identification Numbers). One for the estate; one for the trust. Then direct your executor to dispose of all low-value assets, and compute all tax losses within the nine months of your demise. This way, you accomplish two tasks: (1) settling your estate for Form 706 purposes, and (2) passing the losses through on estate Form 1041. The general scheme we have in mind is portrayed in Figure 7.5.

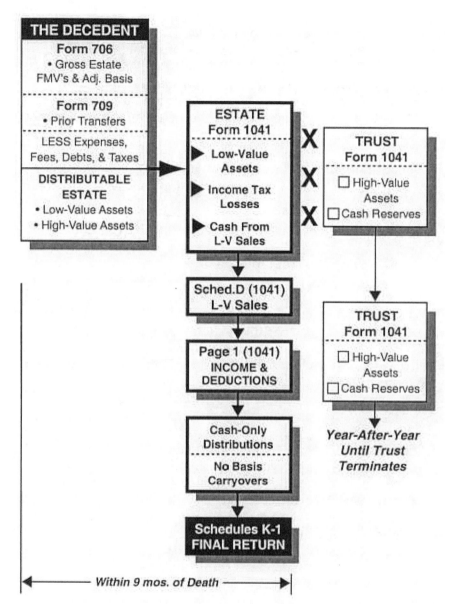

Fig. 7.5 - Rationale for Separating ESTATE Form 1041 From TRUST Form 1041

To help you better understand our thinking, we suggest you read the nine "Yes-No" questions in the *Other Information* section on page 2 of Form 1041. Then read the Schedule K-1 instructions to Box 11: *Final Year Deductions*. Said instructions say—

- *Use Code A for **Excess Deductions on Termination***
- *Use Codes B and C for **Unused Capital Loss Carryovers***
- *Use Codes D and E for **Net Operating Loss (NOL) Carryovers***

Once all of your gross estate accounting is finalized, check the box: ☐ *Final return*, in the head portion (on page 1) of Form 1041. Then start your trust accounting: ☐ *Initial return* for those high-value assets that constitute your distributable estate.

Percentile Your Distributable Estate

The term "distributable estate" pertains to the net portion of your gross estate that is available for distribution to your heirs and others. It is the "net" after diminution for expenses, debts, losses, and taxes. It is also the net after any marital bequest entered on Schedule M or any charitable bequest on Schedule O. Included in the term are the net proceeds from the sale of low-value assets above, and all income and proceeds from high-value property that may or may not be retained in trust.

All beneficiaries, including trusts (if any), should be designated to receive a percentage of your distributable estate. This gives you the flexibility to change your mind at any time, up to the date of your demise. Percentile designation saves you the burden of having to designate specific property items or specific dollar amounts at a time when you have no precise knowledge of what your distributable estate will be. Furthermore, percentiling allows your executor the discretion to distribute property *or* money to accommodate the stated preferences of each distributee.

In an oversimplified way, your distributable estate is—

Your gross estate	$_____
LESS	
• Expenses, debts, & losses	<_____>
• The marital deduction	<_____>
• All related taxes	<_____>

EQUALS
Net amount distributable $ _____

When you use percentile designations, whatever the total distributable amount of your estate may be, can be divided proportionately . . . and painlessly.

For example, you might designate your percentiles as—

Into trust	52%	}
Child 1	16%	}
Child 2	15%	}
Relative 1	10%	} 100%
Relative 2	5%	}
Other	2%	}

You may want to assign only real estate and other income-producing assets to your trust, and direct money and readily convertible-to-cash items to individual persons. This way, there are no carryover basis concerns for individual recipients. In general, most direct heirs prefer cash over property.

Establish a Liquidity Ratio

There's a truly major problem when real estate, stocks and bonds, mortgages and notes, jointly owned property, established businesses, and contemplative-of-death transfers constitute the lion's share of one's gross estate. The result often is that many prospective decedents are "property rich and cash poor." Everything but a small amount of cash to pay monthly bills is tied up in some investment, some commitment, or some arrangement that is not readily convertible to cash. When such a person dies, where does the money come from to pay the estate administration expenses, the debts of the decedent, the transfer and capital gain taxes, and the necessary distribution proceeds?

Answer: It comes from the after-death forced sale of choice assets. When such assets are sold in an estate, rarely is the top dollar (valued in the gross estate) ever achieved. It takes anywhere from 90 days to 180 days, or more, to close some realty transactions. Dismayed by this time lag and by the premature disposition of appreciable property, cash often is raised by refinancing the property while it is in the estate.

Here's a typical situation: a true case. The prospective decedent, a widow, had three multiple-dwelling rental units. They were gross estate valued at—

Property A	— $	850,000
Property B	—	675,000
Property C	—	425,000
Total		$1,950,000

She had cash in the bank of about $20,000. She had nil other assets of value. The rental income was her sole source of livelihood, other than a modest amount of social security. After deductions, expenses, debts, etc., it was estimated that her pre-2010 transfer tax would come to approximately $500,000. Where was she to get $500,000 with only $20,000 cash in the bank?

The answer is that she (or her executor) will have to sell either property A or property B. Yet, she had assigned all properties into trust for her children and grandchildren. This can create a situation requiring probate court intervention.

The long and short is that one must have an adequate liquidity pool within his/her estate, to settle the estate affairs without forced sales of any kind. In the example above, a target liquidity ratio would be 25% ($500,000 transfer tax ÷ $2,000,000 gross estate). We think 35% would be a more comfortable ratio (to allow for outstanding mortgages, debts, and claims). A 35% liquidity ratio means that 65% could be in illiquid assets such as a family business, family farm, or rental real estate.

Organize Your Records

If you pursue none of the suggestions above, the least you should do is organize your estate records for that inevitable day. Organize them for yourself, organize them for your executor . . . while you can. By "organize," we mean arranging them in a systematic and logical manner that makes it easy for your executor to initiate Form 706 within 60 days after your demise. By "organize," we also mean centralizing them in a designated place in your home where they can be found and retrieved easily. A depiction of what we have in mind is presented in Figure 7.6.

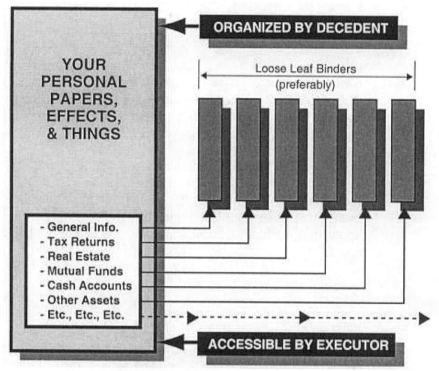

Fig. 7.6 - Setting Your Mind to Organizing Estate Records

As an organizer starter, we suggest that you consider the following separate filing arrangements:

1. General Information

    — birth certificate, military discharge, marriage certificate, divorce decree, educational diplomas, occupational status, retirement letter, prior transfers of property, etc.

2. Relevant Tax Returns

    — all gift tax returns (Forms 709); income tax returns (Forms 1040) and trust tax returns (Forms 1041) for the past five full calendar years; business tax returns (Forms 1065 and 1120/1120-S); Form 706 for predeceased spouse (if any).

3. Real Estate Holdings

— title deeds to real property on which you are named as owner, co-owner, or fractional owner; settlement statements and other documents when property was acquired; installment notes on property previously sold, for which full payment is not yet received.

4. Stocks, Bonds, & Mutual Funds

— latest end-of-year statements on each account in your name, and those identifying other co-owners (other than spouse); include documentation indicating the fractional ownership by others; also include Schedules K-1 for partnerships, LLCs, and subchapter S corporations.

5. Mortgages, Notes, & Cash

— end-of-year cash on hand; end-of-year bank statements, mortgage statements, CDs, T-Bills accounts, savings accounts, etc.

. . . and so on. Use the assets schedules (A through I) on Form 706 as a guideline, and combine items of a similar nature. Have a separate file for debts, credit cards, monthly utilities, and other creditors to whom you owe money.

For ease of organization and retrieval, we suggest using loose-leaf binders with dividers for each different set of records. Storing estate records in mailing-size envelopes, on computer discs, or in a safe deposit box, complicates retrieval and identifying tasks. The advantage of loose-leaf binders is that you are enticed to spread out your records into standard page-reading size of hard copy. Such records can be photocopied easily, for attachment to Form 706 or to any other tax return as needed.

8

CULLING REAL ESTATE

With The Exception Of Your Personal Residence, Holding Multiple Real Estate Properties (5, 10, 15, 20, Etc.) Can Cause Multiple Complications At Time Of Death, AND 6 Months Later. Each Of The 2 Appraisals Requires 3 Pages Of Legal Documentation. For 15 Properties, For Example, 90 Pages Of Attachments To Schedule A (Form 706) Are Required! Organizing Such An Estate Requires Culling Down The Number Of Properties WITHOUT Reducing The Total Gross Value Thereof. This Can Be done Via An Orderly 5-Phase Culling Program, With The End Goal Of ONE MULTI-UNIT Family Business For Your Heirs To Manage.

For some prospective decedents, real estate gets into their blood. There, it becomes a life-long addiction as a means of amassing power and wealth, or at least for building a comfortable nest egg for retirement and old age. Rental real estate is especially addictive in this regard because it—

1. Generates income while being held.
2. Has significant tax shelter benefits.
3. Generally appreciates in value.

These addictive features make it difficult to ever dispose of real estate. There's a sense of power being lost.

There is a common stance among those who have real estate in their blood. Even though one may point out to them the illiquidity of their estate when they die, they are deaf, blind, and immune to any suggestions to lighten up their holdings. Their bristling response is: "It's up to my children and heirs to worry about the illiquidity problem and the tax consequences when I go. This is the way I made my money; this is the way I'm going to pass it along." This *pass it along* attitude is quite typical of multiple-property ownership of real estate.

Aware of this attitude, it is with trepidation that we pose in this chapter ways to lighten the load. For this, our focus is not on disposing all real estate holdings, but on culling through them. The goal is to thin down the number of properties retained . . . to no more than three. One property that should always be retained to the very last is your personal residence. The most desirable properties for retention are multi-unit rentals (commercial or residential) in upscale locations. Other realty holdings such as undeveloped land, odd-shaped lots, farm land, low-income housing, and depleted resource property (cut timber land, abandoned mines, polluted-beach property) are the obvious first candidates for disposal. We offer some constructive culling ideas, if you really want to organize your estate for your heirs.

Canvass Your Children's Wants

Persons with extensive real estate holdings tend to think that real estate being in their blood is also in the blood of their children. This often is not the case. Property owners with more than one adult child may find that not all children have the same desire or financial savvy to inherit real property. In a family of up to five children, we can virtually guarantee that one, two, or three will *not* want your property holdings. They will want money or other liquidity arrangements instead.

Here's a typical, yet true example of what can happen after it is too late. The decedent was the surviving parent (father) of four adult children (three sons, one daughter). His gross estate was approximately $7,000,000 (7 million). Of this, $6,500,000 (approximately 92%) consisted of real estate holdings. All children were to share equally in the estate proceeds. The estate tax on Form 706 approximated $2,500,000, leaving about $4,000,000 potentially distributable to four children.

The oldest son was financially independent on his own. He had his own business and employed his youngest brother in that business. He did not want his share of his father's estate, but wanted to pass it on to his children. His youngest brother desperately wanted the money, as he had recently married and was buying a home (he had a new baby on the way).

The second son and oldest son never got along with each other. Each was in an entirely different occupation. The second son didn't want to be beholden to his financially independent brother. He wanted his $1,000,000 in cash, and he wanted it now! As executor, the oldest son objected. Thereupon, the second son sued the father's estate and was judgment awarded his full share. The attorney and accountant fees amounted to just over $250,000. This reduced the residual estate for the three nonsuing children to about $2,700,000 ($900,000 per heir). The lawsuit caused five years' delay in settling the estate. This caused an additional $600,000 in tax penalties and interest for filing and paying Form 706 late. This further reduced the residual estate for the three nonsuing children to $2,100,000 ($700,000 per heir).

The youngest son, seeing his share of his father's estate diminished by $300,000 ($1,000,000 – $700,000) began to get nervous and concerned. He hinted that he, too might sue the estate for his cash share. The older brother hinted back that the younger brother would be terminated from employment if the estate were sued a second time. In the end, the brother and sister agreed to buy the youngest brother out . . . at some unspecified time.

The example above points up the realities of passing on real estate to multiple children. There is a logical alternative. Canvass them before it is too late, as to their specific choices among your real estate holdings. Prudently feel them out. Which one wants property? Which one wants money? Which one wants to substitute other assets in lieu of his/her share of your real property? Of the children who want your real estate, do they want to own it separately or will they accept co-ownership with their siblings? These and other probing issues should be directed at your children. Take the position that, what may be good for you may not be good for your children. One way to find out is to assign each of your adult children responsibility for managing an entire property unit: interviewing tenants, collecting the rent, overseeing repairs, etc.

Offer to Sell to Children

Canvassing the preferences of your children as above may not turn out to be particularly useful. Your children may not want to offend you, or may not want to appear covetous of your property. They may agree outwardly to accept anything you want to pass on to them, but inwardly they are planning to dispose of it immediately after your demise.

There is a better way of ascertaining the attitude of your children towards real estate. Offer to sell it to them! Make the financial terms of your offer uniquely opportunistic. But make the terms legally enforceable. That is, go through all of the regular appraisal and escrow closing processes. If one or more of your children truly has real estate in his or her blood, an offer of sale is the quickest way to find out.

For example, suppose you have a duplex rental currently market valued at $300,000. You bought the property, or acquired it by exchange more than 20 years ago. It is now paid off and has no mortgage against it. You offer it to all of your children for 5% down (or $15,000). You offer to take back a secured deed of trust note for $285,000. As part of the deal, offer whichever child wants to buy it (and take responsibility for it), a gift of $10,000 towards the down payment. Make sure that you make clear to the nonbuying children that you'll give each of them also a $10,000 cash gift. Money or property gifts up to $12,000 per donor, per donee, per year **are excludable** from your gross estate, and are **not taxable** to the donees thereof [IRS Sec. 2503(b)]. You've probably already heard about this annual exclusion gifting rule, haven't you?

Suppose you die some five years after the one child bought the duplex for $300,000. Its value at time of your death is $400,000. Can't you sense what will happen? The nonbuying children are going to start squawking about the buying child getting a $100,000 inheritance advantage. To a certain degree, that's true. Furthermore, you pay no estate tax on that $100,000. It's a good deal for you, and a good deal for the buying child.

Your nonbuying children need to be reminded that you offered the same deal to them, but they turned you down. They also need to be reminded that when you gave the $10,000 towards the buying child's down payment, you also gave each of them $10,000. What did they do with their $10,000? The buying child "invested" his $10,000 in a parcel of real estate. This is something you had hoped the other children would do, but didn't.

Had you sold the $300,000 rental duplex to your real estate minded child for $15,000 down, you'd be taking back a $285,000 mortgage note. Each year while alive, you would credit that child for $10,000 on principal each year, as part of your annual gift to him. This, together with the child's own payment on principal from his rental proceeds, could drive the balance on principal due down to around $200,000 in five years' time. If you died at that time, the $200,000 unpaid balance would go into your gross estate. This would be in lieu of its $400,000 value had you not sold it to your child. Upon your death, the buying child would inherit the $200,000 balance due note. The note would then be deemed paid in full. Although your other children may grumble about this, they had their chance.

Thus, truly, there are tax advantages both before and after death, when selling real estate to your children. We depict these advantages for you in Figure 8.1. Make sure, however, that there is a bona fide sale, and not a gift disguised as a sale. Also make sure that the transferee child understands Section 453(e): *Second Dispositions by Related Persons* of installment sale property. There is a 2-year prohibition against any resale.

Example of Culling Need

We know it is heresy to make the slightest hint or suggestion that you reduce the multiplicity of real estate holdings in contemplation of your demise. The idea of culling your properties goes against all the conventional wisdom that you have aspired to throughout life. The aspiring wisdom is that you never sell real estate. It is the ancient foundation of wealth and power. Exchange it, if you want, but never sell it. If your children don't want it, put it in a GST (generation-skipping) trust until some grandchild, great-grandchild, or great-great-grandchild somewhere down the line has inherited your savvy and wants to take charge. We are not faulting the wisdom. All we're saying is that you can simplify your estate for passing it down the line by pursuing certain culling effort while alive. "Culling for the future," we call it.

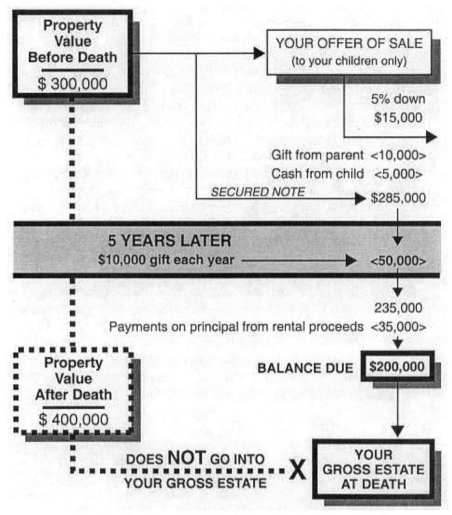

Fig. 8.1 - Tax Benefits When Selling Realty to Your Child

Here's a true example of the need for culling. The decedent and his surviving spouse had 17 separate parcels of real estate. The properties were acquired during their 50 years of marriage. The decedent was a real estate broker, and, after the children became adults, the spouse, too, became a real estate broker. Real estate was truly in their blood. The thought of ever selling any of it was heresy: the total opposite of their inbred beliefs.

All 17 properties co-owned by the decedent and his surviving spouse are listed in Figure 8.2. Be aware that the full appraisal value of each property listed is actually *two times* that amount shown. For listing clarity, we have subtracted the 50% belonging to the surviving spouse. Note that values at date of death and six months after date of death (alternate value: Sec. 2032(a)(2)) are also shown. The data was taken directly from Schedule A (Real Estate) of Form 706 that was timely filed with the IRS within nine months of the decedent's death. The data is NOT fictitious.

Form 706	Estate of: _____ SSN: _____		
	Schedule A - REAL ESTATE		
Item	Description	Alternate Value	Value at Death
1	Personal Residence	110,000	190,000
2	Adjacent Lot #1	81,250	90,000
3	Adjacent Lot #2	81,250	90,000
4	Adjacent Lot #3	37,500	40,000
5	Adjacent Lot #4	32,500	37,500
6	Business Office (Adjacent)	82,500	105,000
7	Rental Property (R-1)	90,000	90,000
8	Rental Property (R-1)	100,000	100,000
9	Rental Property (R-1)	115,000	165,000
10	Rental Property (R-1)	100,000	100,000
11	Rental Property (R-1)	105,000	105,000
12	Rental Property (R-1)	95,000	95,000
13	Rental Property (R-2)	104,000	120,000
14	Rental Property (R-2)	120,000	125,000
15	Rental Property (R-2)	120,000	125,000
16	Rental Property (R-2)	120,000	140,000
17	Unimproved Lot	47,500	60,000
/////	Addresses & parcel numbers omitted	**Total ▶**	1,541,500	1,777,500

Fig. 8.2 - Example (Abbreviated) of Properties Listed on Sch.A (Form 706)

When a Form 706 Schedule A consists of several properties more than the decedent's personal residence, using the 6-month alternate value date is advisable. If the total alternate values turn out to be greater than the date-of-death total values, the higher values can be disregarded. This is the substance of Section 2032(c): *Alternate Valuation Election Must Decrease Gross Estate and Estate Tax*. As you can see in Figure 8.2, the alternate values decreased the gross estate by $236,000 (1,777,500 – 1,541,500). This incurred a tax saving of about $94,000 . . . no small piece of change.

For 17 properties valued on date of death and again six months later, there had to be 34 professional appraisals! For each appraisal, the latest recorded title deed to each property had to be resurrected. In addition, the latest zoning ordinances, environmental restrictions, and building codes had to be at hand. Also, each property had to be physically inspected, as some were over 30 years old. The result was a logjam of paperwork; a lot of physical scurrying around on the properties; and the inevitable differences of professional opinions as to the likely fair market value of each property.

Each appraisal required three legal-sized pages. Page 1 was a detailed description of the property (lot size, building size, type of construction, etc.). Page 2 was a side-by-side summary of at least three "comparable sales" in the neighborhood. Page 3 was a map plot showing access streets and roads and the official parcel numbers assigned by the local assessor. Four different appraisers were used. Altogether, there were **102** (34 x 3) **appraisal documents**! All had to be attached to the Schedule A of Form 706. Seeing this volume of attachments, the IRS accepted the values shown in Figure 8.2. Still, there was a lot of work, a lot of organizing, a lot of time, and a lot of apprehension involved. Had prudent culling taken place before death, some of the agony by the surviving spouse and her children could have been reduced.

The "Never Sell" Plan

The decedent and his spouse had four children: 2 sons and 2 daughters. The decedent had his four young children in mind when he bought his personal residence. He also bought four adjacent lots. Contiguous to these lots, he bought another residence that he converted to a real estate office. His idea was to have his children and their spouses (and his grandchildren) in one contiguous family tract. Upon each child becoming an adult and married, each would be given a parcel of land on which to build his or her own home. This is the "plan" that jumps out at you in the first six items listed in Figure 8.2. At one end of the tract was the parents' residence; at the other end was a residence converted into a real estate office. In between were the four building lots: one for each child. The assumption was that at least one of the children (hopefully more) would become a real estate broker and take over the parents' real estate business.

Here's how things turned out after the death of the father. Only one child, the oldest (a daughter) became a real estate broker. The younger of the two sons was killed as a teenager in a hang glider accident. The other son was not married and had no interest in building a home. The youngest child (a daughter), though married with one infant child, didn't like any of the lots offered to her. She wanted the equivalent value in money to buy an existing home elsewhere. Thus, the older daughter (married) had her choice of the lots and indeed wanted one. Aware of this, the decedent's spouse offered the older daughter all four lots under very favorable financial terms. But she and her husband couldn't come up with enough money to make the minimal 5% down. The daughter decided to wait, and inherit all four lots from her mother.

In the meantime, the local planning commission deemed the lots to be vital public access to nearby coastal beaches. Also, the commission proclaimed the lots to be emergency fire and sewerage line easements, and public access lanes. The surrounding area had built up substantially since the lots were bought (some 40 years prior). The end result was that the four lots had become nonbuildable (for residential purposes) . . . and, therefore, virtually nonsaleable. They became public easement land.

The rest of the decedent's "never sell" plan consisted of six single-family residential rentals and four duplex (two-family) residential rentals. All 14 of the dwelling unit rentals (6 x 1 + 4 x 2) were to go into a business estate trust. This intention created liquidity problems for paying the $350,000 estate tax, and for raising money to remodel and upgrade the properties. None of the children wanted to be responsible for the properties in their present rundown condition. Furthermore, only half of the properties were to go into the decedent's trust. The other half belonged to the gross estate of the surviving spouse. Which half is which? You can't cut a residential building down the middle to make it decedent-trust acceptable. Adding to the dilemma is the fact that the 14 rental units were not of the same value. With professional appraisals, spouses divide the aggregate value: not the number of units.

Do Culling in 5 Phases

There's a moral to the above true life example. You cannot plan the lives of your children, nor the lives of your grandchildren, no matter how admirable your intentions may be. Human minds within the same family are not clones of each other. Each mind acts and thinks differently. The same is true of spouses: each acts and thinks differently . . . especially when anticipating death.

Reality — other than hopes and dreams — requires that you start a culling plan at some appropriate time. The idea is not to diminish the total value of your real estate holdings. Instead, the goal is to reformulate your holdings in a manner that makes directing them into a trust both convenient and expedient. The culling/reformulation process **excludes** your personal residence.

Regardless of your children's likes and dislikes regarding the ownership of rental realty, they all have a nostalgic twinge for the family homestead. Particularly if one or more were raised therein. All individuals reflect back to their pre-adult years . . . with good memories and some bad. Consequently, the family residence is the one piece of property where you'll find easy consensus for co-ownership among your children. It is your one piece of property that is not eligible for culling. You dispose of it only if you intend to retire elsewhere, and need the proceeds for retirement living. Otherwise, retain it until you and your spouse both have deceased. Bequeath it to your children equally. Then leave it up to them to live in it, rent it out, exchange it, or sell it.

Once you set aside your personal residence as a noncandidate for culling, treat all other holdings as full culling candidates. Do so in a logical and orderly manner. We suggest doing your culling in five distinct phases. This will give you time to think through your options, test the current market, and benefit by your one-at-a-time experiences. The five phases that we have in mind *exclude* the preculling phase to your children, which we've already discussed. Preculling enables your children to "show their hand" (as it were) towards property management on their own.

What are the five phases that we propose? They are as follows:

Phase 1 — Sell off all raw land.
- unless you have a binding commitment to build on it or develop it in some manner, sell it.

Phase 2 — Sell or gift low-income and poor quality property.
- gifting to a charitable organization while alive has tax advantages of its own.

Phase 3 — Sell one or more good quality single-unit rentals.
- sell to raise the necessary cash for acquiring one or two multi-unit rentals (of 4, 8, 16, etc. units).

Phase 4 — Exchange your duplex and triplex rentals for one or two multi-unit properties.
- multi-unit properties are more income self-sustaining, and are more attractive for ongoing professional management.

Phase 5 — Designate one multi-unit property for Trust A (for yourself) and a separate multi-unit property for Trust B (for your spouse).
- you have one property to be valued and transferred at death: not dozens.

Our rationale for each of these phases is presented below.

The end goal that you could be focusing towards is summarized in Figure 8.3. Note that your personal residence is not for culling. It will remain in your estate until death. Any property sold to your children will *not* be in your estate at time of death (as per Figure 8.1). This leaves just one target property (a multi-unit rental) for appraisal and its transfer designation. The value of this one property alone could equal or exceed the total value of *your share* of all other properties culled. In total value, you can retain just as much real estate as you want. By having one property instead of 5, 10, 15, or more, your Form 706 is better organized and much simplified.

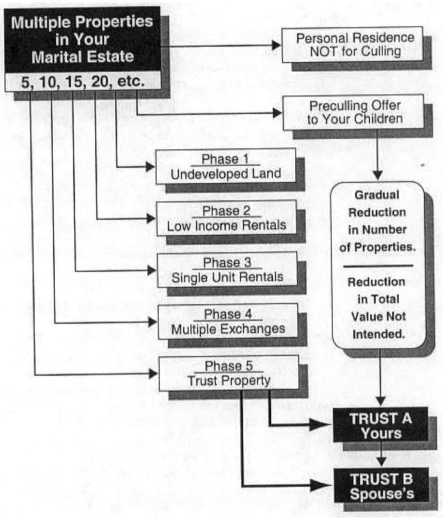

Fig. 8.3 - A "Culling Plan" for Multiple Property Holdings

Phase 1: Undeveloped Land

We have no qualms about your reasons for buying land which is bare, undeveloped, and possibly depleted (of its natural resources). Land is the fundamental ingredient of real estate holdings: residential, commercial, industrial, recreational, etc. Undeveloped land, however, does not produce significant current income. It is *income-producing* property that you want in your final estate. Not some parcel of land that you let some friend park his motor home on, now and then.

Undeveloped land is a drag on your estate. Not only does it clutter your accounting affairs, it ties up money that could be used for acquiring quality income property. It also consumes money in the form of property taxes, weed abatement, trash control, trespassing notices, etc. Our position is: if you have land that you've been holding more than five years, get rid of it! Offer it for sale or auction it; even let it go for property taxes. Rarely can undeveloped land be sold for cash. No one else wants to tie up his money for an uncertain length of time, either. Installment sales are the only practical way to go.

In the example cited above, the decedent actually made two installment sales of land before he died. One such sale was a parcel of commercially zoned land near the heart of a growing community. His share of the sale was $250,000. At the time of death, his share of the installment note was paid down to $228,350. This is the amount that went into his gross estate. No professional appraisal was needed; no alternate valuation was involved. It was a Schedule C (Form 706) asset: Mortgages, Notes, and Cash.

His other before-death land sale was a small lot for $16,500. He gave an interest-only note which he had held for more than five years when he died. The fact that he accepted such a note (no payments on principal) attests to the fact that land is often difficult to sell. This note was included in his gross estate at its initial face amount of $16,500.

Item 17 in Figure 8.2 was also undeveloped land. It was included in the decedent's estate to the tune of $60,000. Its alternate value was appraised at $47,500: a 20% decline.

Phase 2: Low Income Rentals

Having low income rental property means one of two things, or both. One, the property is in such rundown condition that the only way to rent it at all is to charge below market rates. Two, the property is in good condition but is located in a deteriorating neighborhood. Crime, drugs, shootings, rapes, and kidnappings are occurring with increasing frequency. Rarely does low income property reverse course on its own.

Having low income property is often indicative of one's "never sell" philosophy. The property was acquired years and years ago: 30, 40, 50, or more. Its depreciation tax benefits have been used up. The acquisition mortgage is probably paid off. Its basic structure is just so old that the cost of renovation and remodeling would not likely be recovered through rent increases. If it is in your estate at death, it is the most likely to decline in value after death. Such was the case for Item 9 in Figure 8.2. It declined 30% from its date-of-death value ($165,000) to its alternate value ($115,000) six months later.

Low income property is very difficult to sell. Yes, there are potential buyers out there; but, getting a mortgage from a financial institution is not assured. Selling said property on an installment sale is high risk. The risk is in collecting full monthly payments on the note. If the buyer defaults, you — or your heirs — are left with having to take the property back. When you do, its physical condition will be worse — often much worse — than when you sold it, probably at a bargain price.

An alternative is to *gift* the property away. Donate it to a qualified religious, charitable, educational, homeless shelter, or other worthy organization where volunteers will fix it up and maintain it. By a "qualified" charitable entity, we mean one which is IRS-approved pursuant to Section 170(c): **Charitable Contribution Defined**. Preferably make the gift while alive. Have it professionally appraised by using IRS Form 8283: **Noncash Charitable Contributions**. If not while alive, set the designated property up such that there is no question about your donative intent after your demise. Either way, there are distinctive tax benefits for you.

Phase 3: Single Unit Rentals

Culling your property holdings in Phases 1 and 2 is not going to produce much of a cash pool. At best, it will rid your estate of clutter and problem property while you are in control. Even so, you still need a cash pool to acquire quality property in multi-unit form. How are you going to generate this cash pool? Assume that you have multiple property holdings along the lines of Figure 8.2

One way to raise money is to remortgage several of your existing properties to the hilt. Remortgaging can create additional property and financial problems. Each property has to be appraised and risk discounted by the mortgage company. Other property not being remortgaged will have to be pledged as security. If you had six single family rentals, for example (as in the Figure 8.2 case), it is doubtful that you could remortgage more than two or three of them at a given time. Your other low mortgage properties would be held hostage to your remortgaged properties for financial security reasons.

Remortgaging is a good idea *when building up* your real estate holdings over a long period of time. It is not a good idea when culling down your holdings in contemplation of transferring your property holdings to heirs.

Why not consider selling one, two, or three of your multiple single family rentals? A single family unit is relatively easy to sell. It is also relatively easy for the buyer to get a high mortgage. Particularly if the buyer is married and both spouses are employed. In other words, sell for cash-out only. Don't sell under the installment method. Yes, there will be capital gain tax consequences to pay. So, use some of the cash money to pay the taxes. Whatever income taxes you pay before death are NOT resurrected in your gross estate after death. Your estate taxes will be reduced correspondingly: a point to keep in mind.

We already know that our sell suggestion above will not sit well with you. We can hear you asking: "What about a Section 1031 exchange?" In response, we point out that our focus is on simplifying your estate: not on complicating it. We also point out the desirability of an *up*-exchange, for which you'll need a cash pool. An up-exchange invokes no tax consequences at the time.

Phase 4: Multiple Property Exchanges

Phase 4 is a continuation of Phase 3, with a difference. Instead of seeking primarily a cash pool, you are seeking primarily a reduction in the number of properties that you are holding. For this effort, Section 1031 exchanging is the way to go. Chances are, though, one exchange alone will not do it. Phase 4, therefore, contemplates several sequential exchanges. Furthermore, Phase 4 contemplates no payment of taxes, because in each exchange you'll be exchanging UP in property value. You'll be tapping into your cash pool for the up-value differences.

Suppose you had 10 rental properties as in Figure 8.2: six single units and four duplex units. If you'd sold three properties in Phase 3, you'd have seven properties left. Suppose you wanted to exchange these seven properties for one multi-unit rental complex in an upscale metropolitan area? How many exchanges would be required? 2-to-1 and 3-to-1 exchanges are common these days.

A 1-to-1 exchange would get you nowhere. You start with seven properties and would still have seven properties at the end of seven exchanges. You have to think in terms of 2-to-1 and 3-to-1 exchanges. If you can do better than 3-to-1 in a single exchange, go to it. Otherwise, pursue a combination of 2- and 3-to-1 exchanges. You realize, of course, that the more properties involved in an exchange, the longer the processing time required.

Three 2-to-1 exchanges would reduce your property holdings to four (7–1–1–1). Three 3-to-1 exchanges would reduce your holdings to 1 (7–2–2–2). Or, you could make two 2-to-1 exchanges (7–1–1=5) *plus* two 3-to-1 exchanges (5–2–2=1) to get down to a single multi-unit rental property. The number of exchanges you need to make will depend, obviously, on the number of properties you start with, and on the number of properties you want to end up with. Making more than two exchanges in a given year is not advised: too many financial complications. Therefore, plan your Phase 4 exchanges over a period of several years.

Exchanges are ideal when you want to *up-exchange*, which is what Phase 4 is all about. To engage in an up-exchange (where the value of the property acquired is greater than the property conveyed), you need cash and/or other boot. You need the cash and/or boot to equalize the equities (value minus debt) among the properties involved. The term "boot" is property that is not like-kind to those properties being exchanged. To clarify some of the fine points of exchanges that you may have overlooked in the past, we present in Figure 8.4 an illustrative example of "equity balancing." After negotiating this phase of an exchange, let your tax accountant do the rest of the exchange computations for you. Special know-how is required for carryover basis computations.

Step 1	EQUITY BALANCE WITH "BOOT"			
/////////	Properties Conveyed			Property Z Received
Item	A	B	Total	
FMV *	$130,000	$170,000	$300,000	$365,000
Mortgage Debt	<100,000>	<150,000>	<250,000>	<285,000>
Actual Equity	30,000	20,000	50,000	80,000
Boot Required	/////////	/////////	/////////	/////////
- Cash	4,700	5,300	10,000	——
- Other	——	20,000	20,000	——
Balanced Equity	34,700 ●	45,300 ■	80,000	80,000
* FMV = Fair Market Value			"Other" at Fair Market Value	
● = 130/300 x $80,000 = 34,700			■ = 170/300 x $80,000 = 45,300	

Fig. 8.4 - Illustrative "Equity Balancing" for Up-Exchange

Phase 5: Trust Designated Property

Every avid owner of real estate wants to memorialize his achievements made during life. Having built up a substantial estate of realty holdings, he wants to leave some sort of monument for his heirs to see. This is a natural human desire. For satisfying this memorial desire, a trust arrangement has definite merit. Particularly so, if your real estate monument is significant in value . . . say, in the range of $5,000,000 (5 million) or more.

The problem with most trust arrangements is that the property transfer paragraphs are far too generalized. Everything that is not specifically bequeathed elsewhere goes into the trust: all the "pots and pans" (junk real estate) as it were. This is the lazy person's way of creating a trust: assign everything; let the trustee sort things out after the decedent's death. If you have gone through the culling phases above, or intend to, you'll be focusing now on one or more specific items of property that you want in your trust. You want to be most remembered for your organization, expertise, and good judgment in real estate matters. Such focusing is what our Phase 5 is all about.

First off, our position is that you want **one** parcel of quality, multi-unit rental property assigned to your trust. Such property could be a 16-unit apartment building; an 8-unit shopping center; a 24-unit light industrial complex; a 1000 acre farm; a boat marina with 30 docks and slips; or any other property that can be described on a single title deed and given a single parcel number by the local assessor. Thus, the whole idea of Phase 5 is to define and acquire your final property holding for your monument-to-be. Then you spend your active phase-out years improving and sharpening-up your memorial property.

There is just one flaw in our monument scenario. If you are married, does your spouse go along with what you want to be your memorial property? If so, which 50% (or other fraction) is yours, and which 50% (or other fraction) is your spouse's? If the two of you do not agree, your Phase 5 culling should be confined strictly to your own share of the gross marital property holdings. Either way, you need to think in terms of "Trust A" for yourself, and "Trust B" for your spouse. In this manner, each spouse can separately direct the final rearrangement of property holdings as he or she sees fit.

When your Phase 5 effort is complete, and you have perfected your monument, you will have accomplished three major objectives. One, you have "bitten the bullet" and thereby have greatly simplified your transferable real estate. Two, you have assigned income-producing property which is self-sustaining and, thereby, potentially self-perpetuating. Three, if your heirs so desire, after your demise they can down-exchange the multi-unit property into multiple single-family units. Single family units are easier to sell or to occupy, as each heir separately sees fit. With these three accomplishments, you should be proud of the monument that you leave behind.

9

SLIMMING PORTFOLIO ASSETS

> Having Multiple Separate Items Of Paper Assets - 10, 20, 30, 60, Or More - Can Be Exhilarating While Alive . . . And Debilitating After Death. Debilitating Because Each Has To Be Described In 6 Ways On Schedule B (Form 706), UNIT VALUED At Its Market Selling Price, And Share Extended To Whole Dollar Amounts. When No Market Exists, Liquidation Computations Are Required. Tax Exempt Bonds, Foreign Securities, And Domestic Stock Of "No Value" Are Includible In Your Estate. Electing The "Alternate Date" For Valuation Adds Further Complication. Slimming Requires Pre-death Sales And Reporting On Schedule D (Form 1040).

The term "portfolio assets" refers specifically to your holding of variable unit-value securities. The securities are "pieces of paper" representing fractional ownership interests in underlying physical items, such as real estate, corporate enterprises, government activities, natural resources, commodities, and other products of commerce: national and international. Your ownership interests in these items are designated as shares, units, contracts, ounces, barrels, tons, or whatever. Since you are holding paper instead of a chunk of the physical item itself, you own an *intangible* asset. Multiple such ownerships constitute your "portfolio." Ever give thought to slimming your portfolio?

One of the truly attractive features of portfolio assets is that one can amass a quite substantial amount of wealth in pieces of paper alone. Over a lifetime of portfolio accumulations, one can amass in his estate $1,000,000 (1 million dollars), 10 million dollars, 100 million . . . even more. Any such amount can be evidenced by 100 different security issues, or by one security issue alone. The greater the number of security issues outstanding at time of death, the more complicated Form 706 becomes. All portfolio assets are listed and valued on Schedule B of Form 706: *Stocks and Bonds*.

Stocks, bonds, mutual funds, commodity contracts, and various derivatives thereof are bought and sold daily on stock exchanges, on commodity exchanges, and through mutual fund accounts. As a result, portfolio assets can vary in unit price hourly, daily, weekly, or even by the minute, if there is breaking news (good or bad) in the financial markets. This volatility of unit price makes valuing these assets at time of death quite complicated. Although you cannot plan precisely for your date and hour of death, you can take action beforehand to greatly simplify estate matters.

Accordingly, in this chapter we want to focus on techniques and arrangements for slimming down the number of different pieces of paper or accounts in your portfolio. Once we explain the detailed descriptions and valuation procedures necessary for preparing Schedule B (Form 706), we think you'll see some merit to your thinking ahead while alive. Unlike that of real estate (Schedule A/Form 706), you get ample signals and warnings where the complications lie, when you prepare annually your Form 1040. We'll tell you now that if you are a portfolio activist — buying/selling/trading/exchanging on a daily, weekly, or monthly basis — your year of death Form 1040 is one way the IRS has for establishing the validity of that which your executor lists on Schedule B Form 706.

The "Unit Value" Problem

As we pointed out in Chapter 2, there are nine asset schedules that attach to Form 706. All of these schedules require that the value of each listed item be valued *at date of death*. This is mandatory. Additionally, all schedules *permit* an alternate valuation date within six months of date of death for assets actually sold, and *at* six months after date of death for assets not sold. Schedule B, however, is unique among the nine schedules. In addition to the date of death and alternate date values, the **unit value** must be stated for each date . . . for each item listed.

We've already hinted — as if you didn't already know — that stocks, bonds, and other securities experience value changes by the hour: even within the hour in some cases. They certainly change from day to day. This is evident by differences in published high, low, and closing values on any regular trading day. This daily change in unit value raises the question: If a decedent died on a weekend or on a holiday, when the security and commodity markets are closed, which unit value do you use?

For the answer, we have to look to IRS Regulation 20.2031-2(b): *Valuation of Stocks and Bonds; Based on selling prices.* This regulation reads in part—

> *In general, if there is a market for stocks or bonds, or a stock exchange, in an over-the-counter market, or otherwise, **the mean between** the highest and lowest quoted selling prices on the valuation date is the fair market value per share or bond. If there were no sales on the valuation date but there were sales on dates within a reasonable period both before and after the valuation date, the fair market value is determined by taking **a weighted average of the means** between the highest and lowest sales on the nearest date before and the nearest date after the valuation date. The average is to be **weighted inversely** by the respective number of **trading days** between the selling dates and the valuation date.* [Emphasis added.]

Note that this regulation requires the mean value (midpoint) between the highest and lowest value on a designated trading date. This raises the immediate question: Where does one get such values? If the trading date happens to coincide with the valuation date sought, and the security item is published in financial journals or in the business section of general circulation media, use the midpoint of the published high and low, and let it go at that. Keep a copy of the published data for Schedule B backup.

If the valuation date sought occurs when the security markets are closed, the nearest trading dates before and after must be researched. This is where your stock broker, commodity broker, or investment broker can be materially assistive. The value question for Form 706 purposes is a frequent request to brokerage firms dealing in publicly traded securities. You give your broker the name of the issuer of the security, its type and grade, and the valuation date (or dates) that you want. Request a written statement (or computer printout) from him on his firm's letterhead. The IRS rarely questions a brokerage firm's values, if the firm is licensed and if the stock or bond is traded publicly. If an item is not traded publicly, you have work to do.

What If No Market

Not all assets listed on Schedule B are publicly traded securities. Many are "unlisted," "restricted," "private," or "inactive." Most such items are stock shares in closely held corporations, family businesses, and small-issue enterprises where there is just a handful of shareholders. These limited issuances of stock are generally exempt from security registration laws. As such, there is no market where daily quotations can be obtained. And rarely are there any "comparable sales" which can be used as a guide. Now, what?

This is a tough one. You're not going to get any sympathy or help from the IRS. Its suspicion is that you'll undervalue the stock. The IRS wants to see your computations thereon. Its instructions to Schedule B regarding unlisted stock read in part—

Send with the schedule complete financial and other data used to determine value, including balance sheets (particularly the one nearest to the valuation date) and statements of the net earnings or operating results and dividends paid for each of the 5 years immediately before the valuation date.

This is a tall order. You (before death) or your executor (after death) has to compute the value of the private stock as though it were being offered for public registration. That is, you need to use such information as: (1) liquidity ratio (current assets to current liabilities), (2) book value and market value of primary assets, (3) working capital, (4) long-term indebtedness, (5) retained earnings, (6) net worth, (7) voting power of stock if more than one class, (8) history of dividend payments, and (9) ownership preference to assets in the event of liquidation. It is not a matter of computing a reasonable value. Nor is it a matter of referencing some fixed, prior, buy-sell agreement between the principals of the enterprise. It is a matter of computing the *selling price* value . . . in a fair (public) market.

The valuation method most acceptable to the IRS is conducting a *liquidity analysis* of the corporate entity. That is, the corporation is treated as being liquidated for the best immediate cash that can be raised. All salable assets are market valued, all indebtedness is paid off, and a residual net worth is established. Dividing this net worth by the number of shares outstanding gives the value per share. There is no discounting for minority interests, as all stock is treated as being sold simultaneously.

Of all unit value amounts entered on Schedule B, the correctness of the amount for a close corporation is highly controversial. If the number of shares times the unit value exceeds $1,000,000 (1 million), count on the IRS to challenge your valuation. If the extended value is $100,000 or less, your entry would probably be accepted. If more than $100,000 but less than $1,000,000 (extended value), you'd better do your homework carefully. The IRS may request your documentation.

For its instructional benefit, a summary of the principles above is presented in Figure 9.1.

How Many Is Too Many?

Let's assume that you have $1,000,000 invested in common stock. For diversification of risk reasons, such a portfolio amount would require anywhere from 20 to 100 different stock issuers (publicly traded corporations). The exact number of stock issuers would depend on your risk tolerance per issuer. If your risk tolerance were $10,000 per stock, you'd have 100 different stocks in your portfolio ($1,000,000 \div 10,000$/stock). If your average risk tolerance were $20,000, your portfolio would consist of 50 different stocks. For the true life example we have in mind, the decedent had 49 different stocks: $1,297,081 in total value.

In addition to certain risk tolerance, there's also a *complexity tolerance.* In the 49-stock decedent case above, the 85-year-old retired pilot was having endless difficulty keeping track of his stock holdings and rearrangements month to month. The barrage of monthly brokerage statements was just too overwhelming. He seemed confused and bewildered, and made numerous decisional mistakes. This was senility in process . . . and truly sad. But how does one persuade an elderly person to let go?

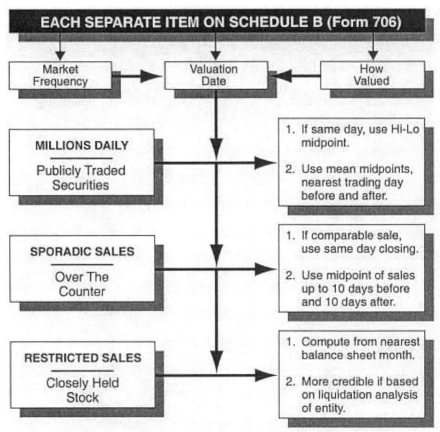

Fig. 9.1 - Establishing "Unit Value" (Selling Price) of Portfolio Assets

When he died, it was necessary to seek the services of a registered financial data corporation to establish the average value per share for each stock holding. The computer results for just nine (of the 49 different stock issues) are presented in Figure 9.2. The data presented are NOT fictitious. For privacy reasons, the name of the decedent, and the 49 names of stock are not disclosed.

Form 706	Estate of _____				
	Schedule B - STOCKS & BONDS				
Item No.	Price * Dates	High	Low	Mean Unit Value	Value at Death
	*Before & after date of death: 01/16/06				
1.					
-					
10.	01/13/06	19.3300	18.8900	19.11000	
	01/17/06	18.7800	18.4700	18.62500	
			1,698 sh x	18.86750 =	32,037.02
11.	01/13/06	33.4000	32.5000	32.95000	
	01/17/06	33.0600	32.3900	32.72500	
			375 sh x	32.83750 =	12,314.06
12.	01/13/06	55.0000	54.3300	54.66500	
	01/17/06	54.8600	54.4100	54.63500	
			200 sh x	54.65000 =	10,930.00
13.	01/13/06	30.9800	30.5300	30.75500	
	01/17/06	30.5200	30.1600	30.34000	
			650 sh x	30.54750 =	19,855.88
14.	01/13/06	45.9800	45.0000	45.49000	
	01/17/06	46.1500	45.0600	45.60500	
			1,250 sh x	45.54750 =	56,934.38
15.	01/13/06	9.7000	9.5000	9.60000	
	01/17/06	9.6200	9.3100	9.46500	
			1,200 sh x	9.53250 =	11,439.00
16.	01/13/06	40.9500	39.9600	40.45500	
	01/17/06	40.7900	39.9300	40.36000	
			1,800 sh x	40.40750 =	72,733.50
17.	01/13/06	74.9600	72.9600	73.96000	
	01/17/06	74.7300	71.5600	73.14500	
			300 sh x	73.55250 =	22,065.75
18.	01/13/06	44.4100	42.9000	43.65500	
-	01/17/06	44.5200	43.0100	43.76500	
-			250 sh x	43.71000 =	10,927.50
-					
-					
49.	Total Shares: 34,790				
//////////////			GRAND TOTAL ▶▶▶		$1,297,081

Fig. 9.2 - Pricing Detail Required When Markets Closed on Date of Death

Even a quick glance at our incomplete Figure 9.2 reveals an astounding fact. To get the *Unit value* for each stock issue (for listing on Schedule B: Form 706) a total of nine "data points" is required. Especially note that the mean values are decimalized to five places! There's also the number of cumulatively-held shares to be established to three decimal places. The number of shares and fractional shares, multiplied by the unit value per share, provides the value of each stock for its: *Value at date of death* listing on Schedule B (Form 706): Stocks and Bonds. Altogether, then, 11 data points (9 + 2) are required for each stock listed on Form 706. Would **you** at age 75 to 85 be able to track this?

For the 85-year-old decedent example above, that would be 539 data points (49 stocks x 11 dp/stock) for entry on Form 706. Can't you imagine the range of possible errors for the Form 706 preparer **and** for the IRS's Form 706 reviewer?

Our reality question is this: How many stock listings on Form 706 are too many? There's no magic answer, of course. The fewer the better. If we were forced to give a number, we'd say five or less. We'd also say, maintain the aggregate total value of holdings that you now have.

Converting to proven-performance mutual funds while alive can provide the ownership diversity of 500 to 1,000 stocks in a single fund. Converting over a 5-year period would be most wise. In our opinion, the conversion should be done no later than by age 75. Otherwise, the tendency is to drift and do nothing . . . and let complexity and disorganization build up.

Descriptive Details Required

Up to this point, we haven't told you what the IRS expects of you — your executor, that is — when describing each stock or bond on Schedule B. The IRS would like to have each stock and each bond identified in seven ways! The prelude to this requirement is the "Description" columnar heading, which reads—

Description including face amount of bonds or number of shares and par value where needed for identification. Give 9-digit CUSIP number.

The CUSIP (Committee on Uniform Security Identification Procedure) is a number assigned to all stocks and bonds traded on major exchanges. For short-term trades, it is rarely used.

Supplemental instructions for describing stocks and bonds on Schedule B read—

For stocks, indicate:
- *Number of shares*
- *Whether common or preferred*
- *Issue* [date, series]
- *Price per share*
- *Exact name of corporation*
- *Principal exchange, if listed*
- *9-digit CUSIP number*

For bonds, indicate:

- *Quantity and denomination*
- *Name of obligor*
- *Date of maturity*
- *Interest rate*
- *Interest due date*
- *Principal exchange, if listed*
- *9-digit CUSIP number*

If the stock or bond is unlisted, show the company's principal business office. If closely held, give entity's EIN.

Do you know the CUSIP number on any of the stocks or bonds you hold? If not, do you know where to find it? It's on your certificates. Very few ordinary individuals hold stock or bond certificates these days. They hold, instead, a "numbered account" with a brokerage firm, mutual fund, or commodities broker. But, suppose you did have your CUSIP number. If you had 49 items to list on Schedule B (as in our example above), that would be 441 digits (49 x 9) to hassle around with and cross-check. In reality, the IRS doesn't insist on CUSIP numbers, except for officers in large corporations. The CUSIPs are primarily for tracking misconduct by major players in the securities markets. For most decedents, with only a few line entries on Schedule B, CUSIPs are not vital and can be omitted.

Still, there are six other descriptive details required for each stock, bond, mutual fund, or commodity contract listed on Schedule B. Continuing with our 49 item example above, there could be as many as 294 descriptive details (49 x 6). Are you beginning to get our complexity point? Our suggestion is to prepare a simple description of each item, attach a more detailed description that you request from your broker, and let it go at that.

The "Accrued Dividend" Problem

Wait! There are still more itemization details required on Schedule B (Form 706). For each item applicable, the accrued dividends (for stocks) and accrued interest (for bonds) have to be included . . . as a separate entry.

The IRS instruction for listing the accruals reads—

*List dividends and interest on each stock or bond separately. Indicate **as a separate item** dividends that have not been collected at death, but which are payable to the decedent or the estate because the decedent was a stockholder of record on date of death. However, if the stock is being traded on an exchange and is selling ex-dividend on the date of the decedent's death, do not include the amount of the dividend as a separate item. Instead, add it to the ex-dividend quotation in determining the fair market value of the stock on the date of the decedent's death. Dividends declared on shares of stock before the death of the decedent but payable to stockholders of record on a date after the decedent's death are not includible in the gross estate.*

Stock dividends are usually declared quarterly, semi-annually, or annually. Interest, by contrast, accrues monthly. Whereas dividends vary, interest is uniform. Consequently, it is when computing the dividend accruals that most of the problems arise. Fortunately, perfect accuracy in your dividend accruals is not so much a virtue as the fact of entering some amount "as a separate item" on Schedule B. Accuracy is not a fetish because the accrual amounts tend to be rather small (order of 1 or 2% or less) of the total value of each stock issue listed. Any "being off a few dollars" is tax treated as *de mimimis*: being immaterial.

In the domain of relatively easy decisions you can make for organizing your estate while alive, we present Figure 9.3. We urge that you look upon Figure 9.3 as a check-off list for actively simplifying your portfolio estate during life. Whatever you accomplish during life does not appear on Schedule B after death.

YOUR PREPARATORY SIMPLIFYING TASKS

1 — Collect all stocks & bonds into one central location

2 — Get rid of all "no value" and worthless stock

3 — Sell off all items whose total value (each) is $100 or less

4 — Batch together all tax exempt state & local bonds

5 — Batch together all foreign securities & foreign tax paid

6 — Identify U.S. stocks paying dividends more than 1%/yr

Fig. 9.3 - The 6 "Easy Decisions" Before Making the Hard Ones

Dispositions Before Alternate Date

Except for stock and debt instruments in close corporations, the items on Schedule B are quite liquid. This is certainly true relative to the liquidity of real estate on Schedule A. Schedule B items, though, are less liquid than monetary accounts on Schedule C. Nevertheless, publicly traded items on Schedule B lend themselves to taking advantage of the alternate valuation date (within six months of death) and its dispositional rules. Once one item on Schedule B is selected for alternate date valuation, **all** items on that schedule (and on all asset schedules A through I), must be valued on the alternate date.

There are three particular alternate date rules that you should know about. These are—

Rule 1 — Items distributed, sold, exchanged, or otherwise disposed of *within six months* after decedent's death.

Rule 2 — Items not distributed, etc. under Rule 1.

Rule 3 — Items whose values are affected by the mere passage of holding time.

In essence, Rule 1 says—

*Any property distributed, sold, exchanged, or otherwise disposed of or separated or **passed from the gross estate by any method** within 6 months after the decedent's death is valued on the date of distribution, sale, exchange, or other disposition, **whichever occurs first**. . . . In the "Description" column of each schedule, briefly explain the status or disposition, such as: "Distributed," "Sold," "Bond paid on maturity," etc.* [Emphasis added.]

Rule 2 simply says that if Rule 1 does not apply, enter in the description column: "Not disposed of within 6 months following death." Rule 3 says that if value is affected by the mere lapse of time after decedent's death, "appropriate adjustments" can be made to the alternate date value.

All that we are trying to bring to your attention at this point is that alternate date valuations — especially for portfolio assets — add complications to your after-death estate affairs. If at all possible, you'd like to simplify matters by "slimming down" said assets. One way to do this is to anticipate what is likely to happen within six months after your demise. If you can anticipate what your executor will do (he/she will have full legal discretion to do whatever is necessary), why not take care of such matters yourself?

Anticipate Via Form 1040

The charge can be made that, to suggest that one anticipate his death, is cruel and inhumane. Yet, we all know that the possibility of death passes through one's mind now and then The passings-through become more frequent as the years decline in number after age 55. In these anticipatory wonderings, the best predictor of what lies ahead in portfolio matters is your own Form 1040: *U.S. Individual Income Tax Return*.

Two particular schedules that attach to Form 1040 are vital Schedule B, Form 706 forecasters. The two schedules are:

Schedule B (1040) — Interest and Dividend Income
Schedule D (1040) — Capital Gains and Losses

It is interesting what these two schedules reveal about the complexity of your portfolio assets before death. They are the forerunner to the transfer of those assets to Form 706 (Schedule B) after death. Let us explain. But first, we caution you: **not to confuse** Schedule B (1040) with Schedule B (706), nor Schedule D (1040) with Schedule D (706). There is no tax relationship whatsoever between these same-lettered schedules on Form 1040 and Form 706. Yet, there IS an anticipatory relationship.

Schedule B (1040) is arranged in three parts. In Part I (Interest Income), you list the interest and OID (original interest discount) that you receive from bonds and other monetary accounts that you hold. In Part II (Dividend Income), you list the dividends and other distributions (capital gains, etc.) that you receive on your stock holdings, domestic and foreign. In Part III (Foreign Accounts), you are asked about your foreign securities and trusts, if any. All of these listings, if not disposed of before death, are the very same items that appear on Schedule B of Form 706. The most likely omissions from Schedule B (1040) are tax exempt bonds, close corporation stock, commodity contracts, and assets that have "no value." These 1040 omissions ARE includible on Schedule B (706). Not only do the extra explanations and statements complicate your Schedule B (706), they imply that you have been inattentive to your financial affairs during life. Slimming down the number of items on Schedule B (1040) before death, translates directly into a slimmer number of items on Schedule B (706) after death. Fewer items mean fewer documents and computations.

Schedule D (1040) presents a different anticipatory role from that of Schedule B (1040). An entry is made on Schedule D (1040): *Capital Gains and Losses*, principally when portfolio assets are sold, exchanged, or otherwise disposed of. If you have no items on Schedule D (1040), it could mean that you have few items to enter on Schedule B (706). Or, it could mean that you have refrained from taking any action to sell or exchange your assets before death. If the latter, you are missing an opportunity to organize and simplify your estate.

If you have numerous entries on Schedule D (1040), it could mean that you are aggressively slimming down your portfolio. Any entry on Schedule D (1040) before death is proof of its sale or exchange for "full and adequate consideration." Any item appearing on Schedule D (1040) before death does **not** appear on Schedule B (706) after death. Using Schedule D (1040) intentionally before death constitutes prudent slimming.

We present in Figure 9.4 a summary representation of the anticipatory roles of Schedules B and D, Form 1040. You may not have thought about these schedules in terms of Form 706 before. They are indeed estate-planning useful, if you put your mind to it.

By "putting your mind to it," we mean reducing your total entries on Schedule B (706) to around five or so (excluding accruals). Towards this end, the role of **mutual funds** is one of the great simplifying achievements of our time. Each fund shareholder participates in *thousands* of portfolio assets with just **one** account. With five such accounts, each with a different investment objective, you can amass all the millions of dollars that you'll ever need for your own life support and enjoyment.

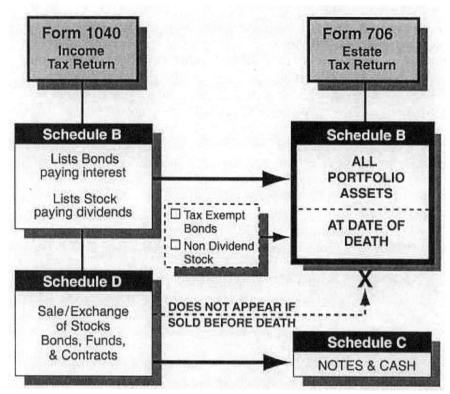

Fig. 9.4 - Anticipatory Role of Form 1040 Schedules for Entries on Form 706

Tax Now (15%), or Tax Later (45%)

Schedule D (1040) serves a distinctive role of its own relative to Form 706. Each entry on Schedule D (1040) could mean that you sold one or more portfolio assets. When such a sale is made, there is a capital gain (or capital loss) income tax to pay. Many prospective decedents refrain from slimming down their portfolios because of said tax. The universal position is: "Why should I pay the capital gains tax; let my heirs worry about that." Is this the wiser choice? Let us examine the matter.

Suppose you held 1,000 shares in the XYZ Corporation which is publicly traded. You bought the shares for $10,000. After several years, the shares rise to $15,000 in value. Do you sell the XYZ stock and pay the capital gain tax on it? Or, do you let the $15,000 be included on Schedule B (Form 706) for estate tax purposes? Assume that your taxable estate (gross minus deductions minus exemption allowance) is over $1,000,000.

If you report the sale of the XYZ stock on Schedule D (1040), you'll have a long-term capital gain of $5,000 [15,000 sales price – 10,000 cost basis]. The capital gains tax rate is 15% (through year 2010). Therefore, you pay $750 in income tax (5,000 x 15%). This leaves you with $14,250 in cash proceeds [15,000 – 750].

Suppose you did nothing with the $14,250. If so, it would wind up in your gross estate on Schedule C (Form 706): **Mortgages, Notes, and Cash**. Your estate tax on this amount would be $6,410 [14,250 x 45% (through year 2009)]. The estate tax starts at 40% for taxable estates over $1,000,000 and increases to 45% for estates over $3,000,000. Together, your capital gain tax ($750) plus your estate tax ($6,410) would total $7,160 . . . almost half of your $15,000 stock value.

Suppose you did nothing before death. That is, you let the $15,000 of XYZ stock go into your estate and be taxed at 45%. The result would be a tax of $6,750 [15,000 x 45%]. This is less than the $7,160 combination above [750 + 6410]. In this case, you are probably right to do nothing.

On the other hand, instead of "doing nothing" while alive, suppose you sold the stock and either consumed $10,000 of it, or gave $10,000 of it to one of your children. Of the $14,250 [15,000 – 750 capital gains tax] after-sale proceeds, your residual cash would be $4,250 [14,250 – 10,000 gift]. You then die, at which time $4,250 goes into your estate. Your estate tax on this amount would be $1,910 [$4,250 x 45%]. Compared to the estate tax of $6,750 above, you have tax saved $4,840 [6,750 – 1,910] on just one during-life portfolio transaction. Furthermore, the $10,000 gift to one of your children is tax free to that recipient. This is a clear case where "doing something" while alive is tax better than procrastinating and winding up doing nothing.

10

BUILDING NEEDED LIQUIDITY

Major Changes In Estate, Gift, And Tax Laws Are Scheduled For Years 2009 And 2010. Until IRS Regulations Thereon Are Promulgated In 2015 (Or So), Planning Uncertainties Loom. For Persons In Retirement With More Than $3,000,000 In Assets, It Is Prudent To Consider Converting 35% Or More Of Your "Excess Estate" Into Cash And Liquid Form. Because HARD DECISIONS Are Necessary, Start The Process At Least 10 Years Before Your Expected Demise. Keep Your Personal Home, Belongings, And Active Business Interests. . . . Then Sell All Else. Do So BEFORE Senile Dementia Sets In. Most Heirs Prefer Cash Over Things.

Liquidity? What is it and why is it needed? Why is it important as an estate organizational tool?

We answer these questions in the order asked.

What is liquidity? Answer: It is having money available to pay your debts when they come due. It is being able to write a check before the deadline without having to borrow money or sell off assets to cover the check. When there's ample "money in the bank," difficult decisions are easier to make on your own (while alive). Liquidity and money are one and the same.

Why is liquidity needed in an estate? **Answer 1**: Before your demise, you need money to pay those professionals whom you engage to prepare various "estate planning" documents; money to pay all living taxes due; and money to make a cash gift or two to family members. **Answer 2**: After your demise, you need money to pay your executor (other than your spouse) and to pay your executor's entourage of "professional assistants"; you need money to pay, or arrange for the payment of all debts outstanding; you need money to pay any and all taxes due (including the estate tax, if any); and you need money to make immediate payments to heirs (other than your spouse) as part of the *closure accounting* and settlement of your estate.

Why is liquidity an organizational tool? Answer: If you truly sense that there is a reason and a need for liquidity in your estate, you'll make some of the hard choices while thinkingly alive to create and build such liquidity. By "hard choices" we mean making those culling, slimming, purging, and related decisions for converting your estate into more liquid form. Such decisions are truly hard because they fly in the face of conventional wisdom, professional motivation, and human procrastination.

Accordingly, in this chapter we want to present our commentary on the liquidity process and why it is so often delayed or not done at all. For this commentary, however, we do make one basic assumption. That is, your gross estate (Schedules A through I of Form 706) is over $1,000,000 (1 million). Although the urgings herein apply to estates of lesser value, only the higher value estates are affected by uncertainties in the estate taxation process ahead. Uncertainty towards the future is good cause alone for building liquidity in one's estate

What are the Uncertainties?

There are four basic types, namely: (1) the estate tax (will there, or will there not be such a tax?), (2) your life expectancy, (3) your health and mental ability, and (4) those always unforeseens.

As of this writing (mid-2006), the estate tax is being phased out, and is supposed to terminate at sunset on December 31, 2009. For this termination to take effect, Congress must expressly pass legislation to repeal the estate tax in its entirety. This would have to take place sometime in 2009: the start of a new U.S. presidential cycle. If total repeal is not enacted, the estate tax is reinstituted and the exemption allowance is reset to $1,000,000 in 2010 (from $3,500,000 in 2009). The only certainty here is that, for estates of lesser value than $1,000,000, the estate tax will be of no concern. For all others, the uncertainty will focus on maximum rates: 35%, 40%, or 45% and on monetary inflationary influences on the exemption allowances. These are the consequences of Public Law 107-16 enacted on June 7, 2001: the start of the current 8-year presidential cycle.

If the 2009 Congress does indeed repeal the estate tax law, the carryover basis rules with respect to property acquired from a decedent after 2009 will apply. We've already discussed these rules in Chapters 5 and 6, previously. These rules mean that your heirs may have to pay tax that you may not have paid. Should you not, therefore, provide some liquidity for them?

Your life expectancy and that of your spouse (if any) can be estimated from IRS-prepared actuarial tables in Figure 10.1. Note that the highest indicated age is 116 years for a female. But also note that the amount of years left in human life runs out fast after 95 (male or female). The actuarial tables alone are no guarantee of how long you will live. This is an uncertainty we all face. To be on the safe side, why not start your liquidity buildup 10 years or more earlier than your actuarial demise?

As to your mental health, who really knows when senile dementia will set in? Such a condition is the normal progression of deterioration in old age. Medical consultation on the state of your mind can be helpful. But it may also be too late to start making the hard decisions for building liquidity prudently. Otherwise, any display of unsound decisional judgments is the frequent cause of probative disputes among heirs and creditors.

And, lastly, there is always some unforeseen event that will drive you wild with liquidity needs. It could be an automobile accident, a natural disaster, an out-of-the-blue lawsuit, an income tax audit, the bankruptcy of your retirement plan, or identity theft. Or, one or more of your children or grandchildren, or those of your siblings, may desperately need money. Do you ignore them, or do you help them with modest cash gifts?

For all of the above uncertainty cases, prudence suggests that you start your estate liquidity program shortly after your retirement years begin. How short is "shortly after"? We think no later than 10 years after your retirement begins. If you haven't achieved the wealth goals that you had hoped by that time, accept your fate. Then move ahead diligently with your estate liquidity objectives.

| AGE IN RETIRE-MENT | LIFE EXPECTANCY | | | |
| | MALE | | FEMALE | |
	Actuarial Factor	Age at Death	Actuarial Factor	Age at Death
50	25.5	75.5	29.6	79.6
55	21.7	76.7	25.5	80.5
60	18.2	78.2	21.7	81.7
65	15.0	80.0	18.2	83.2
70	12.1	82.1	15.0	85.0
75	9.6	84.6	12.1	87.1
80	7.5	87.5	9.6	89.6
85	5.7	90.7	7.5	92.5
90	4.2	94.2	5.7	95.7
95	3.1	98.1	4.2	99.2
100	2.1	102.1	3.1	103.1
105	1.2	106.2	2.1	107.1
110	0.5	110.5	1.2	111.2
115	0.0	111.0	0.5	116.0
/////	IRS Reg.1.72-9 : Annuity Tables		/////	

Fig. 10.1 - Life Expectancy From IRS's Actuarial Tables

How Much Liquidity Needed?

How much liquidity do you need in your estate before senile dementia sets in? This is an unfair question because there's no way to diagnose senility on your own. It is a progressive mental impairment associated with aging. It is a loss of memory concerning one's physical whereabouts and tasks not performed. There's no magic rule of thumb that applies.

We have some thoughts for an answer based on the premise that there's not enough time left in your life to double, triple, or quadruple the current value of your gross estate. With this premise in mind, what would be a respectable target percentage of liquidity in your gross estate?

Do we dare go against conventional wisdom that you've followed all of your wealth building life? Do we dare cross swords with reputable financial advisers who prefer offering you additional life insurance, high-value annuity contracts, managed investment accounts, or participation in tax-exempt "wealth warehousing" schemes? Do we dare horrify you by suggesting that 35% of your gross estate be in liquid form?

Conventional wisdom holds that, if you invest in stocks, bonds, and real estate over the long haul, you will inevitably grow your wealth. The term "long haul" means 10 to 20 years or more. Within this span of time, regardless of the ups and downs of price changes, on average the profit **trend line is up**. This "trend up" wisdom is premised on the fact that price inflation is inherent in the world economy. The fact of life is that there are a limited number of natural resources being sought and consumed by an unlimited growth in human population. More consumers, limited resources, prices up: makes sense, doesn't it?

But, for one whose life expectancy may be sunsetting, continuing with conventional wisdom may not be wise at all. It becomes just another excuse for avoiding the hard decisions. The result is: doing nothing towards building liquidity in your estate.

Certified financial planners have their own take on estate liquidity. Their common theme is to borrow money against your own money in their computerized conventional wisdom programs. If you have life insurance, you can borrow money against its cash value while you are alive. If you have a securities account, the broker managing that account will lend you money by using your account as collateral. If you have real estate, you can always get a line of credit against the equity (value minus debt) in each parcel of such property. But borrowing money against your own money that's already invested is not what we are talking about.

You've got the assets, why borrow against them? Why not — while of sound mind — selectively sell your less profitable assets and receive your own cash to keep on hand? Lots of cash money in an estate is a treasure to behold. It makes things embarrassingly simple when passing cash on to your heirs and to others.

As an absurd example (for making a point), suppose 100% of your gross estate is in all cash form. You live in a retirement home where you pay one monthly sum for food, housing, medical, etc. You have no mortgage or debts of any kind. You have $3,000,000 cash (or readily convertible to cash) in one or more money market accounts. When you die, your executor would have only one asset schedule [Schedule C *Mortgages, Notes, & Cash*] and only one deduction schedule [Schedule J *Funeral & Administrative Expenses*] to complete on Form 706: *U.S. Estate & Generation-Skipping Transfer Tax Return*. Then your executor would check "No" to all the "Yes-No" questions on the form. Whether or not there would be estate tax to pay would depend on the year of death and on the rules in effect at that time.

The moral here is: The more cash you have in your estate, the simpler things will be when settling your estate. You probably never thought in these terms before. Consequently, we suggest 35% or more in cash as a great way to go.

Assign Liquidity Ratings

Building cash liquidity into an estate requires hard decisions. Your very first decision is the hardest. That decision is admitting to and recognizing the necessity to sell assets. Such a decision is hard — very hard — because you are parting from the lifestyle and plan of wealth building that you've been doing for perhaps as many as 50 years in the past.

Once you make such a decision (to sell and rearrange assets), your objective is to build up the cash entirely within your own estate. To meet this objective, you need a plan. That is, you prepare a comprehensive listing of all assets that you possess. List them in any order that is convenient. Then assign to each asset a reasonable market value. You don't need to get professional appraisals at this point. A little inquiry and research on your own is sufficient. All you want is a rough idea of what your gross estate is potentially worth. You want it for decision making purposes: not for actually preparing Form 706.

Once you have listed all of your assets and their approximate values, go through the list and assign to each asset a liquidity rating. A "liquidity rating" is indicative of the relative ease with which you can convert an asset into cash or "money in the bank." We suggest that your most liquid assets be assigned a rating of 1; your least liquid be assigned a rating of 5.

For example, if you have "X" number of dollars in a checking-only account, you know that by writing a check that money is promptly available. We'd assign that asset an LR1 (the "LR" for liquidity rating). Similarly for savings accounts, credit union accounts, money market accounts, certificates of deposit, and other interest-bearing monetary accounts with established financial institutions. Any account that you can liquidate and write a check on the proceeds within 10 days, we'd assign an LR1.

We'd assign other ratings based on the number of days it takes to have check-writing access to the proceeds from asset conversions. The numbers of access days that we would use are:

LR2 — within 30 days
LR3 — within 60 days
LR4 — within 90 days
LR5 — 120 days or longer

Examples of the types of assets that would fall in these categories are presented in Figure 10.2.

As you probably already are aware, business ownership interests and commercial/industrial/agricultural real estate are difficult to liquidate in a short period of time. That's why we assign them an LR5. In short, if your gross estate consists of 50% or more of LR5 assets, you will not only have liquidity problems, but also valuation and tax filing problems.

Management of the Cash Pool

On the assumption that you "buy in" (more or less) to our Figure 10-2-type plan, how do you protect the cash and manage it prudently? On this matter, you have another hard choice to make. Do you open one-only or a multiple of depository accounts? We recommend only one reputable institution of your choice. It could be a mutual fund, a brokerage firm, or a major bank with which you've had satisfactory dealings in the past. Major institutions can handle and protect millions and billions of dollars in cash.

Your cash pool account MUST HAVE check-writing privileges directly tied to an investment choice account. The check-writing subaccount may be of the interest-bearing or non-interest-bearing type (your choice) whereas the directly linked investment account should pay interest, dividends, and/or capital gains (as appropriate to each liquid reinvestment you make).

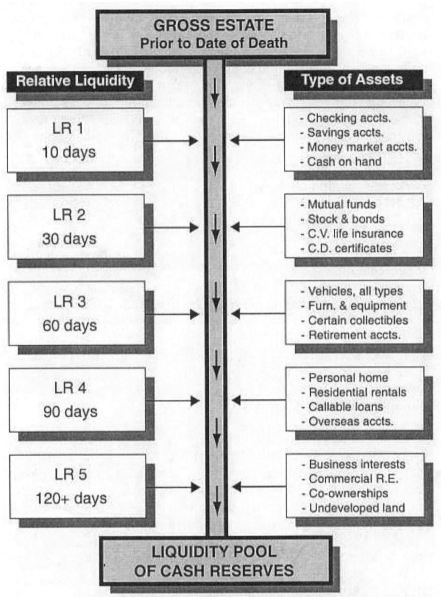

GROSS ESTATE
Prior to Date of Death

Relative Liquidity

LR 1	- Checking accts.
10 days	- Savings accts.
	- Money market accts.
	- Cash on hand

Type of Assets

LR 1
10 days
- Checking accts.
- Savings accts.
- Money market accts.
- Cash on hand

LR 2
30 days
- Mutual funds
- Stock & bonds
- C.V. life insurance
- C.D. certificates

LR 3
60 days
- Vehicles, all types
- Furn. & equipment
- Certain collectibles
- Retirement accts.

LR 4
90 days
- Personal home
- Residential rentals
- Callable loans
- Overseas accts.

LR 5
120+ days
- Business interests
- Commercial R.E.
- Co-ownerships
- Undeveloped land

LIQUIDITY POOL
OF CASH RESERVES

Fig. 10.2 - Suggested Liquidity Ratings for Assets Includible in Gross Estate

The general idea of what we have in mind is schematized in Figure 10.3. Note that there are two distinct pools of funds: a cash pool and a liquidity pool. The cash pool is for immediate check-writing purposes, whereas the liquidity pool is for short-notice (three to five day) conversions to cash. The arrangement depicted can accommodate very large accumulations of cash and liquidity: $1,000,000 (1 million), $5,000,000 (5 million), $10,000,000 (10 million) . . . or much, much more.

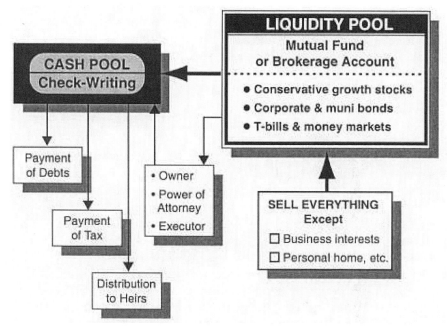

Fig. 10.3 - The "Hard Choices" Plan for Pursuing Liquidity

The next hard choice is: Who is going to control and manage the liquidity plan depicted in Figure 10.3? The owner (or owners), of course, has/have the ultimate control of both pools. But he/they may assign control (**not** ownership) to a designated family member. For such an assignment to have legal effect while an owner is alive, a general power of attorney for business decisions, and a durable power of attorney for medical decisions, should be executed. Designate two separate persons: one for each "power" document. For preparation of the two documents, the services of a licensed paralegal (or of an attorney) should be sought.

There's often a *senility problem* when elderly persons have access to large amounts of cash. In their advancing years, fearing that there's not much time left, they can become squanderers and spendthrifts of their own hard-earned money. They do things they don't recall doing. They keep no records and they don't balance their checkbooks. They are an easy touch for charitable solicitors, and they buy things they don't really need . . . and don't remember buying them. This is a difficult observational phase for caring younger family members who see their "inheritance" being frittered away. The sensible protective recourse is a medical diagnosis of each cash owner's state of mind, supplemented by his or her cooperation in appointing a successor person to handle all financial affairs of the estate.

Estimating Your Estate Tax

One of the priority financial affairs of an estate is to estimate your estate tax. This is quite a different process from estimating one's annual income tax. More importantly, the magnitude of tax in dollars is much greater than that of any income tax payable. For example, if one's *taxable estate* (after deductions and exemptions) is $3,000,000, say, the tax due would be around $1,000,000. For payment of such tax, the IRS will not accept property, securities, collectibles, or other marketable assets. It wants cash. It wants cash in the form of your personal or business check, a cashier's check, an approved electronic transfer, or other instant cash arrangement. Instructions to Form 706 for paying the tax say—

Make the check payable to the United States Treasury. Please write the decedent's name, social security number, and "Form 706" on the check to assist us in posting it [properly].

An "estimate" is just that: an estimate. We can give you a reasonably good approach by shortening the 20 official computational steps on Form 706 to as follows:

Step 1 — Total gross estate $ _____
Step 2 — Total allowable deductions < _____ >
Step 3 — Taxable estate (subtract step 2 from step 1) _____
Step 4 — Total prior taxable gifts _____

Step 5 — Adjusted taxable estate
(add steps 3 and 4) _____

Step 6 — Tentative tax (Table A: Unified
Rate Schedule) _____

Step 7 — Total gift tax previously paid < _____ >

Step 8 — Estate tax before credits
(subtract step 7 from step 6) _____

Step 9 — Maximum exemption credit < _____ >

Step 10 — Net estate tax (subtract step 9
from step 8) _____

A few comments on the above are instructive. Step 1 is the summary of all of your assets Schedules A through I on Form 706, at time of death. If you made any taxable gifts before death, and filed Forms 709, said gifts will be pulled back into your "accountable estate" at Step 4. This accounting pullback is a safeguard against your inadvertently claiming two maximum exemption credits: the one preprinted on Form 709 AND the one preprinted on Form 706. Because the two exemption amounts are different, they are gift-death *unified* via a common tax rate schedule. If you paid any gift tax prior to death, that amount is treated as a *prepayment* towards your death tax (at Step 7). Making prepayments before death via gift tax returns is encouraged as one form of liquidity preparation.

Except for marital and charitable deductions at Step 2, most other deductions (funeral expenses, administrative costs, professional fees, etc.) would rarely exceed 5% of your gross estate. This assumes that, after 10 years of retirement, your mortgages and debts (other than monthly billings) are virtually zero. Thus for estimating purposes (while alive) you can treat Step 2 as being 5% of Step 1.

Role of "Exemption Credit"

At Step 9 above, we use the term: *exemption credit.* Yet, on the official Form 706, the corresponding term is: ***unified*** *credit.* What's the difference?

Answer: In either case, a "credit" is a dollar-for-dollar prepayment against the tentative tax established at Step 6. Note at

Step 6 that we refer to: **Table A** — *Unified Rate Schedule*. The "Table A" is found in the instructions to Form 706 (for estate tax) **and** in the instructions to Form 709 (for gift tax). Since the tax rates are identical for estate taxation and gift taxation purposes, the preferred official term is "unified" credit against either class of tax.

The statutory exemption amounts for estate taxation are reproduced in Figure 10.4. The exemption amount for gift taxation is $1,000,000 for years 2002 through 2010. It thus becomes necessary to convert each exemption amount into an equivalent credit (against tax) amount. The conversion is displayed in the right-hand column of Figure 10.4

We now offer a simple, simple way of estimating your estate tax while alive. We start with the year 2006 because you won't be reading this book before it is published (in 2006). Accordingly, we modify the above steps as follows:

Step 1A — Total gross estate $ _____

Step 2A — Total taxable gifts (if any)   _____

Step 3A — Add steps 1A and 2A   _____

Step 4A — Applicable exemption amount
(from Figure 10.4)   < _____ >

Step 5A — Net taxable estate
(subtract step 4A from step 3A)   _____

Step 6A — Multiply step 5A by 35%,   }
40%, or 45% "as applicable   }
• 35% if less than $1,000,000   }
• 40% if less than $3,000,000   } _____
• 45% if more than $3,000,000   }
Your estimated (while alive) estate tax _____

Whatever you estimated while alive estate tax may be, it is not payable until after your demise. We suggest that you not wait until then. So, go ahead and use our simple 6-step computational sequence above, and come up with your own estimate. Especially for gross estimates in the above $3,000,000 range, one should have a good handle on what his estate tax would be, if he were to die in years 2006, 2007, 2008, or 2009.

Nor is the estate tax payable and due until nine months after your demise. At that time, Form 706 must be prepared and filed.

If the 706 return — NOT the payment — cannot be filed on time, an automatic six-months extension of time to file can be obtained. For this extension, IRS **Form 4768** is required. Part IV of this form is bold captioned:

Payment to Accompany Extension Request

There are no grace periods or interest-free periods after nine months after your demise. Can you sense now why we advocate that at least 35% of your gross estate be in cash form while alive?

For Decedents Dying During --	Exemption Amount	Equivalent Credit Against Tax
2000 & 2001	$ 675,000	$ 220,550
2002 & 2003	1,000,000	345,800
2004 & 2005	1,500,000	555,800
2006, 2007, & 2008	2,000,000	780,800
2009	3,500,000	1,455,800
beyond 2009	??	??
Sec. 2010 - Unified Credit Against Estate Tax Subsec. (c) - Applicable Credit Amount		

Fig. 10.4 - Applicable Exemption Amounts & Conversion Credits for Estates

Years 2010 and Beyond?

If you are alive in years 2010 and beyond, there are certain uncertainties to think about. Will there be an estate tax for those years or not? If there is one, what will be its exemption amounts and tax rates? Will the estate, GST (generation skipping transfer), and gift taxes be repealed in their entirety, or will there be some residual form of GST tax? The GST tax is currently a separate add-on tax computation of its own and conceivably could be an extension of the current GST policy. It is a very complicated tax to compute (requires a 5-page Schedule R of Form 706), for which its complexity alone is a just reason for repealing it.

If the estate, gift, and GST taxes are indeed repealed, will there be some equivalent substitute tax?

Obviously, we have no better answers than you with respect to the above uncertainties. The best we can do is to think ahead in terms of Scenario 1 and Scenario 2. Scenario 1 assumes that the estate tax is reinstated at a fixed lower exemption amount and at a fixed maximum tax rate. Scenario 2 assumes that the carryover basis rules apply, and that some form of prepayment credit will be allowed to recipients of property who subsequently sell it. Our rationale for these two scenarios is portrayed in Figure 10.5.

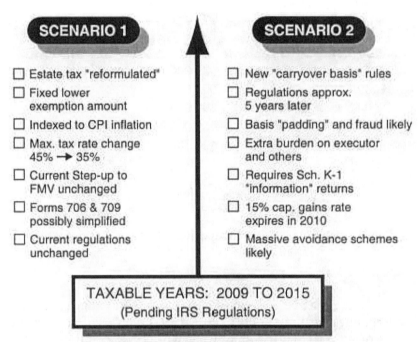

Fig. 10.5 - The Uncertainties Ahead for Estate Planning & Organization

As we understand the situation, the year 2010 is expected to be a major transition year in *transfer taxation* policy. Our use of the term "transfer" taxation includes all forms of transferring property gratuitously to others for less than full and adequate consideration (in money or money's worth). When ownership of property is transferred without sufficient consideration, grandiose opportunities are created for tax evasion, fraudulent schemes, and illegal scams. Hence, some form of transfer accounting at the federal level must be anticipated. Putting emotions and politics aside, our humongous federal deficit alone will dictate that some form of responsible transfer accounting will be instituted. What form? We don't know. That's why we explore (in Figure 10.5) two different scenarios for years 2010 and beyond.

Scenario 1: Form 706 Simplified

It is unrealistic to anticipate that Congress will eliminate gift, estate, and GST taxation in its entirety. It is realistic, however, to hope that maybe — just maybe — Congress will simplify the transfer accounting process. By "simplifying," we mean a more uniform and consistent way of computing the tax on page 1 of Form 706. This IRS form is truly a complicated piece of work due to no fault of the IRS. Its complication is caused by special-interest enactments for family businesses, family farms, family and GST trusts, conservation easements, and terminable interest properties. Somehow these worthy causes need to be preserved.

One way to achieve some simplicity in Form 706 is to fix the exemption amount and reduce the progressive tax rates that apply. Then uniformize everything: gifts before death, bequests upon death, and skips after death down generational lines.

A fixed exemption amount: How much? $1,000,000 (one million); $3,000,000 (3 million); or $5,000,000 (5 million)? Whatever Congress devises, fix it at one amount and leave it alone for at least five years. Do not inflation index it. This way, estate owners can plan their property transfers more sensibly.

As of this writing, the fixed exemption amount stands at $1,000,000 (for year 2010), and the maximum tax rate is set at 35% (for year 2010). The estate tax rate schedule appears to be heading into graduated rates of from 15% to 35%, which are more or less in line with personal income tax rates.

If Scenario 1 were to be the case, one's gross estate at time of death would include—

- All assets at hand, unsold $_____
- Certain pre-death gifts   _____
- Transfers in GST trusts   _____

          Grand total gross estate ▶ $_____

From the total gross estate, all previous type deductions (expenses, fees, debts, mortgages, losses, etc.) would be allowed. In addition, worthy cause deductions could be allowed. The "worthy causes" would be those mentioned above re special interest enactments (and possibly others). All allowable deductions would subtract directly from the total gross estate to arrive at an adjusted gross estate.

From the adjusted gross estate, the fixed exemption amount would be subtracted directly. There would be no exemption credit conversions whatsoever. The result would be one's *taxable estate*. The tax rate structure — as suggested here — could range from a low of 15% to a high of 35% (maximum). The 15% rate could apply to taxable estates in the range of $1,000,000 whereas the 35% rate could apply to taxable estates exceeding $10,000,000 (10 million). In other words, once one's taxable estate exceeds $10 million, the tax rate would be **flat thereafter**. On this premise, the wealth dynasties would bear their fair share of the federal revenue burden (since they have derived the most benefit from it).

Scenario 2: Carryover Basis

As things now stand, Public Law 107-16 (enacted 6-07-2001) provides that—

Beginning in 2011, the estate, gift, and generation-skipping transfers taxes are repealed. After repeal, the basis of assets received from a decedent generally will equal the basis of the decedent (i.e., carry-over basis) at death. However, a decedent's estate is permitted to increase the basis of assets transferred by up to a total of $1.3 million. The basis of property transferred to a surviving spouse can be increased (i.e., stepped up) by an additional $3 million. Thus, the basis of property transferred to a surviving spouse can be increased (i.e., stepped up) by a total of $4.3 million. In no case can the basis of an asset be adjusted above its fair market value. For these purposes, the executor will determine which assets and to what extent each asset receives a basis increase. The $1.3 million and $3 million amounts are adjusted annually for inflation occurring after 2010.

The above wording is the legislative forerunner of IRC Section 1022: *Treatment of Property Acquired from a Decedent Dying after December 31,2009.* This 2,000-word tax law mandates that a carryover basis be established for all property items exceeding $1,300,000 in a decedent's estate. This mandate is reinforced by new Section 6018: *Returns Relating to Large Transfers at Death* (about 500 words). We covered these two tax code sections quite thoroughly in Chapter 5: Carryover Basis Rules and in Chapter 6: Post 2009 Thinking, and prefer not to repeat the same points here.

As we ourselves reread subsection 1022(e): *Property Acquired from the Decedent* and subsection 6018(c): *Information Required to be Furnished* (re property transferred by decedent), your executor is mandated a heavy carryover basis burden. As we've said previously, basis records on long-held property are poorly kept, if kept at all. Memory recall is often the best that one can do.

Back in Figure 7.3 (on page 7-12), we gave a true-life example of memory recall for basis reconstruction purposes. Without memory recall, the only documented basis was $125,000 (as stepped up from a prior decedent). The property actually sold for $1,600,000. That's a potential $1,475,000 taxable gain! Can't you sense the opportunities for "basis padding" by executors who try to appease the grumblings of heirs and beneficiaries? In Figure 7.3, the basis padding — as it would be called by the IRS — amounted to $402,703. Would the IRS accept an undocumented basis adjustment of this amount after a decedent's death? Whether it would or not, what's to prevent outright carryover *basis guessing* in order to minimize downstream taxation?

As of this moment, subsection 1022(h): **Regulations** reads—

The [IRS] *shall prescribe such regulations as may be necessary to carry out the purposes of this section.*

Once a new law goes into effect, it takes about five years before any regulations are published. This takes us to the year 2015 or so before any regulations against carryover basis padding, guessing, memory recall, or fraud can be promulgated. In the meantime, each property owner while alive, or each executor after the owner's death, must, in good faith, do the best that he or she can to reconstruct basis records.

Back to: "Cash is King"

Whether or not Scenario 1, Scenario 2, or neither comes into being, there are just too many estate planning uncertainties ahead. This is because year 2009 will be a crucial year for the Nation as a whole: politically, morally, and financially. Unless the FMV of your gross estate is less than $1,300,000, the IRS is going to get a cash payment from you in one form or another. It could be an estate tax, a carryover basis tax, a gift tax, or a capital gain tax. It would be naïve to believe that Congress would intentionally abandon or repeal all forms of transfer taxation after one's demise.

This gets us back to our soapbox for building liquidity slowly and purposely into your estate. Doing so means warehousing the cash in readily accessible form. We schematized this pursuit previously in Figure 10.3. Now we want to add one more tidbit of wisdom to our earlier portrayals.

Strictly for illustration purposes, let's assume that your gross estate is greater than $3,000,000. You are 10 years into retirement and are 75 years old. Our Figure 10.1 actuarial table indicates that you'll probably live 10 more years. To consume your $3,000,000 over a 10-year period, what would your annual consumption rate be? Answer: $300,000 per year ($3,000,000 ÷ 10 years). If you lived another 10 years (to age 95), your annual consumption rate would be $150,000 per year. Could you not live on this amount in your twilight years?

All of which brings us to our crescendo point. If you have an estate exceeding $3,000,000, why not sell the entire excess and convert it to cash? We mean this! With so many transfer tax uncertainties ahead, why not convert your entire "excess estate" into tax-free municipal bonds issued for the state of your residence. Talk to your financial advisor or to your mutual fund broker about this. Have an arrangement whereby you — or your executor — could instantly write a check for $100,000 or $1,000,000 . . . or whatever. Your heirs will have fonder memories of you than if you burdened them with carryover basis rules, regulations, and returns . . . which they probably wouldn't understand. Everybody understands cash; it has no carryover basis.

11

FILING GIFT TAX RETURNS

> Gifting While Alive Not Only Organizes Your Estate Better, It Enables You to "See For Yourself" Threefold Tax Benefits. These Include: (1) The $12,000 PER DONEE Annual Exclusion (Without Limitation On Number Of Donees), (2) Partial Or Full Use Of The $1,000,000 Exemption Credit, And (3) The Documentation Of Donor-To-Donee CARRYOVER BASIS Information On Which You Pay No Tax. Each Form 709 Is A PER DONOR Return (Even If Married) And Is Prepared For Each Calendar Year Of Tax-Accountable Gifting. It Requires The Listing of Each Donee's Name, Relationship, And All Prior Year Taxable Gifts.

One of the least understood and most underused documentation of gratuitous transfers is the gift tax return: **Form 709**. The gift tax — like the estate tax — is a tax for the privilege of transferring property to others for less than full and adequate consideration. The type of property covered is real or personal, whether tangible or intangible, made directly or indirectly, in trust, or by any other means. The gift tax is a transfer tax in exactly the same sense that the estate tax is a transfer tax. It is NOT an income tax nor is it a property tax. The gift tax is in effect through year 2010.

Back in 1976, Congress *unified* what were previously two separate tax rate schedules, and two separate exemption amounts, into one package. As a result, the gift tax rates and the estate tax rates are identical. The exemption amounts, though unified, are not identical. The applicable gift or estate exemption amount is *per individual*, whether living or deceased. There is one transfer tax exemption amount during life and (currently) a higher exemption amount at death. This way, the portion unused during life is automatically available for use at time of death.

The gift taxing rules have one unique feature which the death taxing rules do not have. The first $12,000 of a gift is not taxed; it is an *exclusion*. Furthermore, it is an *annual* exclusion [IRC Sec. 2503(b)]. Still further, a gift of $12,000 can be made to any number of donees (recipients) by a single donor, in a given year, and no gift tax applies. For example, if you had five children, siblings, or relatives, you could gift away $60,000 . . . without tax. If you made the gifts five years in a row, you could gift transfer $300,000 without tax.

If married at the time of each of the five separate gifts, in five sequential years, your spouse, too, could transfer $300,000 without tax. Between the two of you as separate donors, you could transfer legitimately $600,000 out of your combined gross estate. Still, each of your separate lifetime exemption amounts ($1,000,000 per spouse) would remain intact!

Failing to use the role of gift tax returns in estate planning endeavors stems from the term: "tax return." People just don't like filing tax returns. Believe it or not, this one type of return can be used advantageously to both *simplify* and *reduce* your gross estate when your final day comes. This is because the gift tax return has a **cumulative accounting feature** which no other IRS return has.

Consequently, in this chapter we want to acquaint you with Form 709: ***U.S. Gift (and Generation-Skipping Transfer) Tax Return***, and explain how it can be used for recording and compiling all of your estate plans and strategies. The key in this regard is the use of Schedule B on Form 709: ***Gifts from Prior Periods***. Our contention is that a file of Forms 709 provides a documentation trail that is authentic and convincing. Such a file removes the suspicion of tax avoidance, should any of your prior transfers be silent, insufficient, or inadequately documented.

Death Bed Usage

It is standard procedure when the IRS examines a death tax return (Form 706) to request a listing of all gifts made within three years of death. The IRS requests the names of all persons to whom gifts were made, whether more than $12,000 or less than $12,000. For the less than $12,000 gifts, the IRS requests some documentation of each such gift. It wants to see a letter of gift intent, an affidavit of acceptance, a canceled check, a bank statement of deposit, an electronic transfer confirmation, or whatever else is appropriate to dispel IRS suspicion. Without convincing documentation on the nontaxability of gifts for $12,000 or less, the IRS has no choice but to presume that, potentially, hordes of cash and/or property may have disappeared, underhandedly, from the decedent's gross estate.

There is also a "standard procedure" in human nature. When death is imminent, or likely to be so, there is a mad dash — the death bed syndrome — to gift away money and property. Most such gifting is not properly documented. The attention and focus are on reducing the prospective decedent's gross estate as rapidly as possible. Heirs and relatives encourage this procedure. Rarely does any heir or relative think of documenting each gift via a gift tax return. Let us illustrate the typical scenario with a true case.

A widower had two daughters and five grandchildren: totaling seven donees. He gifted each of them $12,000 in each of the three years before his death. These gifts reduced his gross estate by $252,000 (7 x $12,000/yr x 3 yrs). Though his estate was reduced, the gifts were not made properly.

Each year he wrote two checks. One check went to Daughter A for $36,000 ($12,000 for herself and $12,000 for each of her two children). The second check went to Daughter B for $48,000 (herself and three children). Instead of there being seven nontaxable gifts each year, there were two *taxable* gifts: one for $24,000 [36,000 – 12,000] and the other for $36,000 [48,000 – 12,000]. Despite professional advice to the contrary, each daughter wanted the checks written as stated. Each wanted to control the money gifts to their own children. Thus, in IRS eyes, there were NOT seven gifts each year; there were only two such gifts. Both were taxable. And since no gift tax returns were filed, the amount of $180,000 ([24,000 + 36,000]/yr x 3 yrs) was added back into the widower's gross estate when he died.

In a situation like the above, preparing a gift tax return becomes the ideal document. Each year, the donor prepares one

Form 709 and lists on it the name, address, and relationship of each of the seven donees. For the amount of gift to each, he enters $12,000. Over a 3-year period that would be 21 gifts of $12,000 for a total of $252,000 (21 x $12,000 each). Thus, each gift would have been properly reported to the IRS — and properly excluded — on the proper document, namely: Form 709.

Overview of Form 709

Now that we have exemplified the benefits of Form 709 as a prima facie document of your gift transfers, let us overview the form with you. Officially its full title is: *U.S. Gift (and Generation-Skipping Transfer) Tax Return.* Note the parenthetical inclusion of "generation-skipping transfer," or GST for short. In other words, Form 709 is applicable for gifts to your parents, to your siblings (of your same generation), to your children (one generation below you), to your grandchildren (two generations below you), to your great-grandchildren (three generations below you), and to others yet unborn down your generational line. Our contention is that Form 709 can address all of your wealth transfer intentions while you are alive, even though some of those intentions may not be carried out until after your demise. Such is the role of "generation skipping."

Form 709 is filed on a calendar year basis. It consists of four pages of statements, columns, and lines. This number compares with 40 pages for Form 706: the estate tax return. Form 709 is accompanied by 12 pages of official instructions, compared with 30 pages for Form 706. For prior transfer accounting purposes, Form 709 covers everything that Form 706 covers. Indeed, a very prominent question on Form 706 asks:

Have Federal gift tax returns ever been filed? □ *Yes* □ *No.*
If "Yes," attach copies of the returns and furnish: (a) Period(s) covered, and (b) Internal Revenue office(s) where filed.

In highly abbreviated and outline form, the contents of Form 709 are listed in Figure 11.1. The appearance of complexity stems predominantly from generation-skipping transfers (GSTs). If one postpones his GST intentions until later in life, Form 709 boils down to page 1, plus Schedule A and Schedule B, only. This is the situation for most ordinary transfers of money and/or property.

Form 709	U.S. GIFT TAX RETURN	Year
	Name, Address, & Tax ID of Individual Donor	

Page 1

   • Part 1 - General Information . . . [18 lines]
   • Part 2 - Tax Computation . . . [20 lines]

Page 2   SCHEDULE A

☐ Computation of Taxable Gifts . . . [22 lines, 5 columns]
   • Part 1 - Gifts Subject Only to Gift Tax
   • Part 2 - Gifts Subject to BOTH Gift Tax & GST Tax
   • Part 3 - Gifts of Indirect Skips to Trusts

Page 3

   • Part 4 - Taxable Gift Reconciliation

SCHEDULE B

☐ Gifts from Prior Periods . . . [5 lines, 5 columns]

Page 4   SCHEDULE C

☐ Computation of Generation-Skipping Transfer (GST) Tax . . . [22 lines, 5 columns]
   • Part 1 - Generation-Skipping Transfers
   • Part 2 - GST Exemption Reconciliation
   • Part 3 - Tax Computation

Fig. 11.1 - General Contents of Form 709 for Each Individual Donor

Of particular note, which is not evident in Figure 11.1, is that Form 709 is a **per individual** return. It is not a husband and wife return, even if married at the time of each gift transfer. This is so, even though provisions on the form allow for *gift splitting* between husband and wife. An instruction to this effect says—

*A married couple may not file a joint gift tax return. However, if after reading the instructions below, you and your spouse agree to split your gifts, you should file **both** of your individual* *gift tax returns together (in the same envelope) to avoid correspondence from the IRS.*

The gift splitting rules between spouses are hairy for combined gifts in excess of $24,000. Consent and cross-consent portions of the form have to be addressed and signed. We suggest, therefore, that you disregard the gift splitting lines on Form 709. Each of you prepare your own return, independent of the other. Each spousal gift return becomes an attachment to Form 706 when each spouse deceases. There is no joint estate tax return, even if both spouses die simultaneously in the same event.

Transfers Subject to Form 709

In the broadest general sense, Form 709 accommodates all conceivable forms of gratuitous transfers. It covers all transfers by gift whether present interests are given, or future interests are given. A gift is a *present interest* if the donee has all immediate rights to the use, possession, and enjoyment of property and its income. A gift is a *future interest* if the donee's rights to the use, possession, and enjoyment of property and its income will not begin until some future date.

The present vs. future distinction is important with regard to the annual exclusion of $12,000 per donee. Gifts of present interest are allowed the exclusion, whereas gifts of future interest are not allowed the $12,000 exclusion. Also, future interests require revaluation of the gifted amount when said interests "trigger in." The gift of a present interest to more than one donee as joint tenants in property, or as joint beneficiaries in a trust, qualifies for the annual exclusion for *each donee.*

As to the actual types of transfers subject to being reported on Form 709, selected excerpts from the official instructions say—

The gift tax applies not only to the gratuitous transfer of any kind of property, but also to sales or exchanges not made in the ordinary course of business, where money or money's worth is exchanged but the value of the money or money's worth received is less than the value of what is sold or exchanged. . . .
The exercise or release of a general power of appointment may

be a gift by the individual possessing the power. . . . The gift tax may also apply to the forgiveness of debt, to interest-free loans, to the assignments of the benefits of an insurance policy, and to the giving up of some amount of an annuity in exchange for the creation of a survivor annuity. . . . Transfers to family members of interests in corporations, partnerships, and trusts are gifts. The lapse of any voting or liquidation right is a gift.

And so on. It is hard to find any gratuitous transfer of property or money which is not subject to gift tax accounting, where the gross amount to any one donee exceeds $12,000. For example, municipal bonds that are exempt from federal income tax are *not* exempt from federal gift tax. Nonresident aliens gifting tangible property located in the U.S., whether to a U.S. citizen or to a foreign citizen, are subject to filing Form 709.

There are two types of transfers that are not subject to Form 709. These are payments to: (1) educational institutions for tuition, and (2) health care providers for medical expenses [IRC Sec. 2503(e)]. To the extent that a payment is for other than educational or medical use, it is a gift to the individual on whose behalf the payment is made.

Schedule A, Part 1 Listings

The head portion on page 1 of Form 709 requests certain information about the donor, such as whether he died during the year, etc.. One particular item is a statement that reads—

Enter the total number of separate donees listed on Schedule A. Count each person only once. ▶ _____

The message behind this statement is that you have to start at Schedule A before any gift tax can be computed. If, for example, you entered 3 in the space above, the processing assumption by the IRS would be that no tax would apply to the first $36,000 of your gratuitous transfers. Keep in mind that Form 709 is prepared for each full calendar year: one year at a time. Each year for which you file a Form 709, the $12,000 annual exclusion per donee applies (if "present interests" are conveyed).

As Figure 11.1 indicates, Schedule A is titled: ***Computation of Taxable Gifts***. Below this title is Part 1 which is subtitled: ***Gifts Subject Only to Gift Tax***. Between this title and subtitle (not indicated in Figure 11.1), there is a preprinted question:

Does the value of any item listed on Schedule A reflect any valuation discount? Yes ☐*, No* ☐*. If the answer is "Yes," attach explanation.*

This is your tip-off that the IRS is apprehensive, rightfully, about your intentionally undervaluing nonmarketable property interests. Unpleasant tax penalties can be imposed. So, beware!

Undervaluation improperly leads to conservation of the unified (exemption) credit. Consequently, the essence of the instructions regarding valuation discounts is—

*If the value of any gift you report in Schedule A reflects a discount for lack of marketability, a minority interest, a fractional interest in real estate, blockage, market absorption, **or for any other reason**, answer "Yes" to the question [above]. Also, attach an explanation giving the factual basis for the claimed discounts and the amount of discounts taken.* [Emphasis added.]

Once you get past the above question, Part 1 of Schedule A consists of eight columns. These columns are lettered:

A — Item number
B — Donee's name, address, relationship to donor, and description of gift
C — Disregard (applies only to GST direct/indirect skips)
D — Donor's adjusted basis of gift
E — Date of gift
F — Value at date of gift
G — Disregard (applies to splitting gifts with spouse)
H — Disregard (net of Col. F minus Col. G)

Columns C, G, and H add unnecessary complexity. Columns B, D, E, and F are where all the *disclosure action* lies.

Before describing your disclosure actions more fully, the format of Schedule A is instructive. Said format is presented in Figure 11.2. Note that we have omitted Columns C, G, and H. Also note that Column B takes up most of the horizontal white space. This implies that the information you enter in Column B must be full and complete. Instructions say that—

If you need more space than that provided, attach a separate sheet, using the same format as Schedule A.

Schedule A	COMPUTATION OF TAXABLE GIFTS		Form 709	
Part I	GIFTS SUBJECT *ONLY* TO GIFT TAX			
A	B	D	E	F
Item No.	• Name, address: Each Donee • Description of Gift	Donor's Adjusted Basis	Date of Gift	VALUE at Date of Gift
		Total Gifts		
		Per Donee Exclusions	<	>
		TAXABLE GIFTS		

Fig. 11.2 - General Format of Part I, Schedule A, Form 709

Columns B, D, & F Explained

Column B requires that each donee be separately listed by name, address, and Tax ID (social security number for individuals and EIN for trusts). Corporations and partnerships do not qualify as donees of gratuitous transfers. The Column B instruction for trusts says—

If the gift was made by means of a trust, enter the trust's identifying number [EIN] and attach a [stamped recorded] copy of the trust instrument.

Professionally prepared trust instruments can be quite voluminous: 35 to 50 pages on average. Therefore, use good judgment and attach only the vital pages that describe each beneficiary and his or her relationship to the donor. If, as the donor, you make transfers to more than one trust, your transfer accounting life will be complex. Make sure that you carefully distinguish the EINs.

From what we've told you previously about carryover basis rules, you surely must know that whenever there is any transfer of property, the IRS wants to know the *identifying numbers* of all parties involved. This is so that its computer can cross-match that which a transferor reports, with that which a transferee reports. Accordingly, list all names and IDs of individuals in a chronological order by age: oldest first, youngest last. If there is more than one transfer to the same donee, list the present interests first, then the future interests.

Column B also requires a description of each transfer to each donee. The instructions for the descriptions say (in part)—

> *Describe each gift in enough detail so that the property can be easily identified. . . . For interests in property based on the length of a person's life, give the date of birth of the person. . . . For life insurance policies, give the name of the insurer and the policy number.*

Other instructional descriptions parallel those on Form 706 for its nine asset schedules: A through I. Recall Figure 2.2 (on page 2-7) and the asset descriptions in Chapter 2. A point to keep in mind is that whatever you distribute after death can be pre-distributed during life as a gift.

Column D in Figure 11.2 is headed: *Donor's adjusted basis of gift*. One's "adjusted basis" in property is his acquisition cost (or other basis) plus additions, less allowances for depreciation, amortization, and depletion (if any). Only the donor has these records; the donee does not. In the case of a gift, the donor's basis is transferred to the donee . . . along with the property. This basis information is needed, should the donee subsequently dispose of the property in a taxable transaction.

Also in Figure 11.2, Column E is headed: *Value at date of gift*. The valuation instructions at this date are identical to those instructions on Form 706 for "Value at date of death." All valuations entered on Form 709 or 706 must be supported with full information on how each value was determined. Whether one transfers an interest in property during life or at death, it has to be fair market valued on the date of the transfer.

Prior Gifts on Schedule B

Schedule B of Form 709 is titled: *Gifts from Prior Periods*. Obviously, if you are preparing Form 709 for the very first time, you will have made no prior gifts. You can skip Schedule B. But, if you make a taxable gift any prior year, Schedule B must be used. You'll see the rationale for this, when we explain its columns.

Schedule B has five columns: A, B, C, D, and E. Unlike Schedule A, however, the columns in Schedule B are functionally different. You can sense the difference in the headings below:

A — Calendar year (of prior gift)
B — Internal Revenue office where prior return was filed
C — Amount of unified credit against gift tax for periods after December 31, 1976
D — Amount of specific exemption for periods ending before January 1, 1977
E — Amount of taxable gifts

Column A shows the year in which a Form 709 was previously filed. If five prior Forms 709 were filed, for example, there would be five separate calendar year entries. List chronologically, starting with the farthest year back.

Column B asks for the IRS office where you filed each of your prior year Forms 709. This means that you should have kept a copy of each of your prior returns. Each such return gives your name, address, Tax ID, and other information which the IRS keeps in its data base as far back as 1970. Gift taxing is a cumulative process. The result is that each subsequent gift pushes you higher and higher up the gift-death tax rate schedule and uses up more of your exemption credit.

Column C carries the cumulative tracking concept further. Corresponding to each year in Column A, you enter the amount of exemption credit that you claimed for that year. You obtain this amount from page 1 of each prior Form 709 at the line marked: *Unified credit* [applied]. At the bottom of the column, you show the cumulative total of all prior year exemption amounts. At some point, you may exhaust the maximum exemption allowable.

We will skip over Column D. For our readers it is inapplicable. It applies only to a short specific period of time before 1977 when the gift tax and estate tax rates and exemptions were "unified." We have long since passed that period.

Column E (amount of taxable gifts) is the bottom line of Schedule A for each prior Form 709. The term "taxable gifts," recall, is the total market value of actual gifts, less the annual exclusion for each donee listed in Schedule A. There is no reference in Schedule B to any prior donees. This is because it is the *donor* who has to pay the gift tax: not the donees.

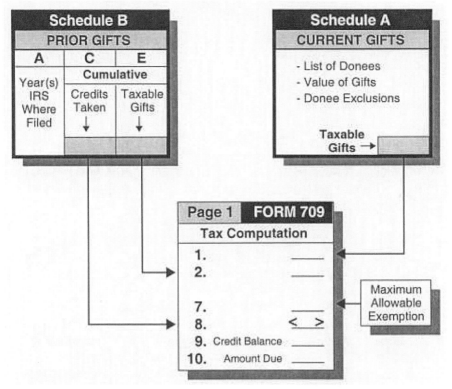

Fig. 11.3 - The "Prior Gifts" Accounting Role of Schedule B on Form 709

In Figure 11.3, we portray the interrelationship between Schedule B (for prior years) and Schedule A (for current year). We also show how the two are totaled on page 1 (tax computation) of your current Form 709. Particularly note how the cumulative prior exemption credits *subtract* from the maximum allowable exemption amount for the current year. The difference is a *credit balance* that can be used over several years of lifetime gifting.

Tax Effect of Prior Gifts

Gift taxing invokes a unique concept of its own. Unlike income taxing which is a separate year tax, gift taxing is a *cumulative* tax. As successive year gifts are made, all prior taxable amounts are added to the current year taxable amount. At this point, a cumulative tax is determined. From this cumulative tax, all prior year taxes are subtracted. This gives the current year gift tax. There **is** a valid rationale for cumulative gift taxing.

The estate tax is a transfer tax on your accumulation of wealth throughout all of your years of living. If you made no gifts during life, your estate tax would be one gross-up figure. If you made a series of gifts (without the effect of cumulative taxing), your estate tax would be substantially lower than if no gifts were made. In effect, you would get two exemption credits instead of one. Whether a family recipient acquires property by gift or by inheritance, its tax character is the same. It is a *gratuitous* transfer for which no consideration is paid. Being of the same character means that only one exemption applies. Hence, Congress prescribed that the gift tax and the estate tax be unified and equal. The only way to achieve this "unification" was to require that gifting be cumulatively taxed, rather than being separately taxed each year. In this manner, every individual is free to make gifts or not make gifts, as he or she sees fit. The tax rates and exemption credits favor neither gifts nor death.

The cumulative gift taxing process is best explained by abbreviating the 20 computational steps on page 1 of Form 709. About half of these steps require tangential explanations which distract from the focus of our discussion. By omitting these tangential matters, the gist of the page 1 *Tax Computations* is reduced to 10 steps as follows:

Step 1 — Current year taxable gifts $_____
         (from Schedule A, after exclusions)

Step 2 — Prior year taxable gifts   _____
         (from Schedule B, Col. E)

Step 3 — Cumulative total taxable gifts   _____
         (add steps 1 and 2)

Step 4 — Tax computed on step 3   _____
         (from Form 709 instructions)

Step 5 — Tax computed on step 2   _____
         (from Form 709 instructions)

Step 6 — Current year gift tax   _____
         (subtract step 5 from step 4)

Step 7 — Maximum unified credit $345,800*
         (preprinted on Form 709)

Step 8 — Cumulative prior credit allowed   _____
         (from Schedule B, Col. C)

Step 9 — Unused balance of credit   _____
         (subtract step 8 from step 7)

Step 10 — Current tax due (if any)   _____
          (subtract step 9 from step 6)

*Equivalent to an exclusion amount of $1,000,000 [IRC Sec. 2505(a)(1)].

Last Chance for Annual Exclusions, Etc.

Whereas the estate tax is scheduled to terminate after December 31, 2009, the gift tax is scheduled to terminate after December 31, 2010. In other words, the gift tax terminates one year later than the estate tax. Then, commencing in 2011, the carryover basis rules apply across the board to all forms of gratuitous transfers: during life, at death, and down generational lines. The carryover basis rules are premised on taxing the *basis spread* (between FMV and basis transfer) at capital gain rates. This has been the practice with gift transfers since 1977.

What will change with respect to gift transfers commencing in year 2011?

For one thing, the annual exclusions will be eliminated. An "annual exclusion" is a subtraction from the total value of gifts made during the taxable year. Such exclusions are subtractable year after year; there is no cumulative total subtraction limit. For example, a donor can give $10,000 a year to each of 10 donees for each of 10 years. If so, the cumulative result would be $1,000,000 ($10,000/yr x 10 donees x 10 yrs) worth of exclusions.

The most common annual exclusions are those prescribed in subsection (b): *Exclusions from Gifts*, of Section 2503: *Taxable Gifts*. The key wording of subsection 2503(b) reads—

> *In the case of gifts . . . made to **any person** by the donor **during the calendar year**, the first $10,000 of such gifts* [inflation increased re 1997] *to such person **shall not** . . . be included in the total amount of gifts made during such year.*

Editorial Note: For year 2006, the per donee per year exclusion is $12,000 after adjustment for inflation. This amount is a pure gift; there are no strings attached if no "future interests" are involved.

The whole purpose of Form 709 is to report your taxable gifts to the IRS. The process therewith on its Schedule A, Part 4 — *Taxable Gift Reconciliation*, goes like this—

1. Total value of gifts by donor $_____
2. Total annual exclusions   <_____>
3. Total included amount of gifts (subtract line 2 from line 1)   _____

If the gift tax is repealed/terminated/eliminated as is presently scheduled, there is no further tax accounting recognition of any annual gift exclusions. Such being the case, the period 2006 through 2010 (five years) is your last opportunity — last chance — to use IRS Form 709 for estate planning advantages. We urge, therefore, that if you've never filed Form 709 before (and even if you have), that you actively engage in a 5-year program of Form 709 filings . . . to reduce your gross estate at time of death.

There's also a second grand-chance last opportunity for an estate advantage with Form 709. There's a built-in $1,000,000 maximum *exemption* against all of your cumulative taxable gifts. The "exemption" applies to all taxable gifts after the annual exclusions are subtracted out. If you make $100,000 in taxable gifts five years in a row, for example, that would be $500,000. When you do the gift tax computations (which we abbreviated via 10 steps on page 11-14), the result is still no gift tax.

Hence, our message is this. Why not take advantage of the $1,000,000 gift tax exemption while alive? This assumes that you have a gross estate of at least this amount . . . preferably more.

There is just one catch to our $1,000,000 gift urging above. Whatever the value amount of your taxable gifts, whether taxed or not taxed (when being $1,000,000 or less) is added back into your estate at time of death. Thus, for best estate results, do your "large gifting" in years 2006 through 2009 (four years instead of five). This is because your estate tax exemption is $2,000,000 in years 2006 through 2008, and $3,500,000 in 2009. It is reset to $1,000,000 in 2010 so as to reconcile with the gift tax exemption of the same amount.

Unlike an estate tax return which is filed within nine months of your demise, gift tax returns are filed on a calendar year basis. This means a due date on or before April 15th of the year following each gift year. We see no reason for these due dates being altered in the future. There will always be some kind of reporting of gifts.

Additionally, by filing Form 709 for large gifts, you are automatically adapting to the post-2010 carryover basis rules. As we indicated in Figure 11.2, there's a distinctively separate column officially captioned: ***Donor's adjusted basis of gift.*** Our expectation is that for years post-2010, Form 709 will be reformulated and recaptioned possibly as: *U.S. Gift (and GST) Information Return* (in lieu of "tax" return). The fact that there may be no gift tax applicable after 2010 provides now a unique and special opportunity (pre-2011) that you ought not to miss!

12

INITIATING YOUR OWN 706

The FORM 706 EXPERIENCE Is A Rarity Among Taxpayers While Alive. It Unfolds ONLY When Actually Filling Out The Form, Starting On Page 1 At Line 1: Decedent And Executor. Other Parts Are 3: Elections By Executor, And 4: General Information. Part 5: RECONCILIATION Can Be Filled Out After Schedules A Through I (ASSETS) And Schedules J Through U (DEDUCTIONS) Are Completed. If "Generation-Skipping Transfers" Are Made, Schedules R and R-1 Are Required. Part 2: TAX COMPUTATION Is The Last To Be Filled Out. Net Distributive Amounts Are Entered In Part 4 To "Top Off" The 706 Experience.

The "706" refers to IRS **Form 706**. Its short title is: *U.S. Estate Tax Return*. The term "estate" refers to your property holdings and interests that remain unconsumed at the time of your death. The term "tax" is the liability assessed against your estate for the pure privilege of passing/transferring your property to others . . . gratuitously. The preparation and filing of Form 706 applies generally to gross estates over $1,000,000. This filing threshold increased to $1,500,000 for years 2004 and 2005; increases to $2,000,000 for years 2006, 2007, and 2008; and to $3,500,000 for death year 2009.

We have cited above only the "short title" of Form 706. Its full title is: *U.S. Estate (and Generation-Skipping Transfer) Tax Return*. Definitely note the word "**and**" in this long title. This word means that IN ADDITION TO the estate tax, there is a GST tax. The two taxes — estate tax and GST tax — are added together near the bottom of page 1 of Form 706. In previous chapters, we have not said much about the GST tax. It is a very complicated tax, targeted primarily at wealth having $100,000,000 estates or more. We'd rather focus on lesser wealth estates, somewhere under $10,000,000 or so.

In order to expand your knowledge and enhance your appreciation of Form 706, we offer a novel approach. WE WANT **YOU** TO INITIATE THE PREPARATION OF YOUR OWN FORM 706! To our knowledge, no one else has ever suggested that a prospective decedent do this. This is not a wacky idea at all. It makes good sense. It is the best way in the world to really know what your executor has to endure when you are gone. Why not share in your executor's duties now?

Accordingly, in this chapter we want to whisk you through Form 706 in its entirety. Obviously, we cannot expect that you totally complete the form and sign your own name to it. That's for your executor to do. Nevertheless, you can prepare a *comprehensive draft* of it. Then include the draft with other important papers in your estate file. Doing so will put you many steps closer to reality than your contemporaries.

Fill Out Part 1 on Page 1

The best way to gain familiarization with Form 706 is to start filling it out! We mean it. Fill out Part 1 on page 1. Below the form title, Part 1 comprises about two vertical inches of space. It consists of 14 entry spaces. All but two or three of the entries can be completed by you.

The title of Part 1 is: ***Decedent and Executor***. You are not the decedent — not yet, anyway — and you are not the executor. Still, we want you to start filling out the form as though you were both decedent and executor. This will give you a different perspective of what your afterlife will be.

The first three entry blocks in Part 1 are:

1a *Decedent's first name and middle initial (and maiden name, if any)*
1b *Decedent's last name*

2   *Decedent's social security number*

The mere fact of thinking like an executor for a decedent puts you in an entirely different frame of mind when addressing a tax form.
The next four entry blocks are:

3a   *Legal residence (domicile) at time of death*
3b   *Year domicile established*
4   *Date of birth*
5   *Date of death*

Obviously, you can't fill out your own date of death. You have to leave item 5 blank. Whatever that date turns out to be, it has to be corroborated by attaching a certified copy of your death certificate.
The next three entry blocks pertain to your executor. They are:

6a   *Name of executor*
6b   *Executor's address*
6c   *Executor's social security number*

If you have updated your will, as we urge you to do, fill in these blocks now. In your will, you have to designate your executor and his/her successor. The instructions for ***Name of Executor*** say—

If there is more than one executor, enter the name of the executor to be contacted by the IRS. List the other executors' names, addresses, and SSNs on an attached sheet.

The next two entry blocks are:

7a   *Name and location of court where will was probated or estate administered*
7b   *Case number*

If **all** of your assets were in joint tenancy with your spouse, or in joint tenancy with one or more of your adult children, or in a revocable living trust, you could enter N/A (Not Applicable) in these two blocks. We suggest otherwise; leave **7a** and **7b** blank. You really do not know whether your estate will be probated.

Much depends on the savvy and self-reliance of your executor and on the recalcitrance of your heirs and their attorneys.

Three Checkboxes in Part 1

The last three entry blocks in Part 1 read:

8   *If decedent died testate, check here*   ▸ ☐
and attach a certified copy of the will.

9   *If you extended the time to file this*
Form 706, check here   ▸ ☐

10   *If Schedule R-1 is attached, check here*   ▸ ☐

If you are not already familiar with the term "testate," it means: *having made and left a legally valid will.* With an estate in excess of $1,000,000 up for grabs, surely you have an updated will, do you not? So, check the box at item 8.

An application for an extension of time (beyond the statutory nine months) to file Form 706 is made on Form 4688. Our thesis throughout this book is premised on no extensions. Allow yourself and your executor six months to get the return done and pay any applicable tax. You have a cash and liquidity pool, don't you? So, leave the box at item 9 blank.

The checkbox at item 10 cannot be addressed until you complete Schedule R: *Generation-Skipping Transfer Tax*, as well as Schedule R-1: *Direct Skips from a Trust*. The preprinted instructions on the back side of Schedule R-1 say, in part—

> *Schedule R-1 (Form 706) serves as a payment voucher for the GST tax imposed on a direct skip from a trust, which the trustee of a trust must pay. The executor completes the schedule and gives 2 copies to the trustee. Both the executor and trustee sign the R-1s and attach one copy to Form 706 with a check or money order . . . payable to the "United States Treasury."*

We'll address Schedules R and R-1 very briefly later; meanwhile, leave the box at item 10 blank.

Now that you have completed Part 1 as much as you can, skip over Part 2: *Tax Computation*. You can not complete Part 2 until you have completed Parts 3, 4, and 5, and all schedules on Form 706. There are nine asset schedules to complete (A through I) and seven deduction schedules (J through U). Schedules R and R-1 are not deduction schedules. The next part that you can do is Part 3: *Elections by the Executor*.

Four Elections by Executor

Part 3 (at the top of page 2) consists of four rather technical questions. You **and** your executor may have to do a little research on these questions. By "research" we mean studying the IRS instructions that relate to the questions, and reviewing the applicable sections of the Internal Revenue Code. The four questions, as they appear on Form 706, consist of approximately 65 words. The IRS instructions thereon comprise about 4,800 words. The applicable IR Code sections (2032, 2032A, 6166, and 6163) consist of about 11,000 words. Obviously, you cannot — should not — answer these questions off the top of your head. Each requires a checkbox answer: ☐Yes, or ☐ No.

In abbreviated form, the questions read as follows:

1. *Do you elect alternate valuation?*

2. *Do you elect special use valuation?*

3. *Do you elect to pay the taxes in installments?*

4. *Do you elect to postpone part of the taxes?*

As to Question 1: alternate valuation, we suggest a "No" answer. The alternate valuation law (IRC Sec. 2032) says that you can revalue everything up to six months after death. Our premise is that, if you have done the simplifying efforts that we have proposed in previous chapters, you should be able to complete the entire Form 706 in six months' time. Simply instruct your executor to sell everything that he needs to *before* the six months, and treat the proceeds amount as the date of death value.

As to Question 2: special use valuation, do you have a family farm or family business of which more than 50% is "qualified real property" (of more than $750,000 in adjusted value)?. If "Yes," the instructions tell you to prepare Schedule A-1: Section 2032A Valuation. This schedule and its instructions take up six pages on Form 706. Glance through these pages and read the 20-step checklist for this election. If you do not have a qualified family business, then "No" will be your answer.

As to Question 3: installment payments, your answer might be "Yes," or it might be "No." It depends on there being any closely held business (proprietorship, partnership, or corporation) in your estate that exceeds 35% of the value of your gross estate. We see merit in a "Yes" answer if your estate truly has illiquid assets to the extent described in IRC Section 6166: *5-Year Deferral 10-Year Installment Payment.* If you are one owner of a 5-owner successful business, would you want to force its sale and closure just to pay your death tax?

As to Question 4: postponement of taxes, we suggest a "No" answer. The postponement rule of Section 6163 applies only to reversionary or remainder interests. These are ownership interests covered by Section 2033 (any interest at time of death) and Section 2037 (transfers taking effect at death). Subsection 2037(b) defines the term "reversionary interest" as—

Any possibility that property transferred by the decedent [before death] *may—*
   (1) return to him or his estate, or
   (2) be subject to a power of disposition by him [at death].

With all of the preplanning and simplifying efforts that we have urged upon you previously, you should feel quite comfortable with a "No" answer to Question 4.

Importance of "Letters Testamentary"

The questions in Part 3 above (and others in Part 4 below) require that your executor make probing inquiries into your estate affairs. His inquiries are going to generate hostility and taunting by prior transferees, asset holders, financial institutions, out-of-state sources, and out-of-country authorities. Beneficiaries and their attorneys are going to be particularly hostile. To these persons, presenting them with a copy of your will (or a copy of your trust) appointing your executor will not convince them of his authority. They want to see a court-approved legal document called: *Letters Testamentary*. A college dictionary definition of this term is—

A written instrument from a court or officer thereof informing an executor of his appointment and of his authority to execute the will of the decedent.

How does your executor get Letters Testamentary?

Answer: He has to petition the Superior Court, Probate Division, for such letters in the county where you reside. Each state has its own petitioning process and legal forms. The type of initiating legal form is: *Petition for Probate of Will, Letters Testamentary, and Independent Administration* . . . or other title words to this effect. On the petition form, your executor requests via checkboxes that—

a. ☐ Decedent's Will be admitted to probate.

b. ☐ He be appointed Executor with Letters Testamentary.

c. ☐ Authority be granted to administer estate independently.

d. ☐ Bond not be required.

Other matters also appear on the petition form. The principal such "other matter" will be a public *Notice of Death and of Petition to Administer Estate*. The Notice is addressed to all heirs, beneficiaries, creditors, contingent creditors, and other persons who may have a financial interest in the will or the estate of the decedent. A hearing date is set, after which — if there are no objections or challenges — the presiding judge affixes his signature to an *Order for Probate*. Thereupon, the court clerk issues the Letters Testamentary. This one-page document is typified in Figure 12.1. That presented is a preprinted legal form for the State of California, which can be procured by nonattorneys.

	For Court Use
Petitioner's Name:	
Address: Business Hours Phone No.	
SUPERIOR COURT OF _____ COUNTY OF _____ Address:	
Estate of _____ Decedent _____	Date of Death:
LETTERS TESTAMENTARY	Case Number:

1. ☐ *The Last Will of the above named decedent having been proved, the court appoints*	4. AFFIRMATION *I solemnly affirm that I will perform the duties of personal representative according to law.*
_____ ☐ Executor	Executed on _____ At _____ ____/s/____ Personal Representative
2. ☐ *The court appoints* _____ ☐ Administrator	
3. ☐ *The personal representative is authorized to administer the estate under the Independent Administration of Estates Act* ☐ WITH full authority ☐ WITHOUT authority to *sell or exchange real property*	5. CERTIFICATION *I certify that this document is a correct copy of the original on file in my office, and that the letters issued the above-appointed person have not been revoked, amended, or set aside, and are still in full force and effect.* Date: _____ _____, Clerk by _____, Deputy
OFFICIAL SEAL	OFFICIAL SEAL

Fig. 12.1 - Near-Replica of Official Form: Letters Testamentary

We can hear your cries of anguish now. "You mean *my* estate has to be probated? I have everything in joint tenancy; I have a living trust; I'm covered by insurance and other contracts. My attorney has assured me that no probate will be necessary."

Our position is that for any estate exceeding $1,000,000 your executor should be *prepared* for probate. He doesn't actually have to complete the process; just initiate it. There are a lot of dissidents out there who will try to disqualify your executor, if he doesn't petition for Letters **within 30 days** after your death. The term "out there" includes stalking attorneys, disgruntled heirs, activist professionals, and recalcitrant asset holders. A several million dollar plum hanging from a tree is a natural target for covetous pickers. Picking at and fee-milking such a plum is a form of legalized grave robbing. It happens more often than you realize.

So, get your executor prepared. In fact, **accompany him** to your county law library, to the superior court probate clerk, and to the legal forms publisher in your area. Get sample petition forms and pleadings. After a petition for letters case has been heard, that case's records are open to public inspection. You and your executor should inspect several such records in the probate clerk's office. Seek permission for photocopying, and pay whatever clerk's fee is necessary. The procedures and hearing on a petition for Letters Testamentary are quite perfunctory. No attorney is needed. Only if your will is contested, or your executor is charged with malfeasance of duty, is an attorney required.

Overview of Part 4

Now, back to Form 706 and its Part 4: *General Information*. Items 1 through 5 of Part 4 are matters that relate to your occupational background, marital status, and amount of dispositional intent. Item 1 reads:

Death certificate number and issuing authority (attach a copy of the death certificate to this return).

Obviously, you have to leave item 1 blank. As to items 2, 3, 4, and 5 you can certainly fill those in.

Item 2 asks for your business or occupation, or former business or occupation. Item 3 asks for your marital status (including date of divorce and date spouse predeceased you, if applicable). Item 4 asks for your surviving spouse's name, social security number, and the amount that you have specifically bequeathed to her. Item 5 asks you to list: *Individuals (other than surviving spouse), trusts, or other estates who receive $5,000 or more; Identifying number; Relationship to decedent; and Amount.*

We urge that you fill in items 4 and 5 completely. Read the instructions carefully, and enter all names and dollar amounts. There's a *Total* in the amount column which should reconcile with your *distributable estate.* The amount distributable is your gross estate after subtractions for deductions, expenses, and taxes. Estimate these amounts the best you can, then come back later and refine them.

General Information: Continued

Items 6 through 16 of Part 4 are quite technical and detailed. Each item requires a "Yes/No" checkbox answer. In some cases, research of the applicable tax law and extensive inquiries to your heirs, transferees, and custodians of property will be required. Somewhere in the process of answering these questions, presentation by your executor of his Letters Testamentary will be required . . . and possibly challenged. You can help to reduce any post-death discord that might arise by doing pertinent research and inquiry on your own, while alive.

We urge that you read through all of the questions yourself. Better yet, you and your executor go through them together. Skim-read them first, for orientation purposes. With Form 706 in front of you, start at the top of page 3 which is headed: *Part 4 — General Information (Continued).*

Preprinted bold instructions to Questions 6 through 16 say—

Please check the "Yes" or "No" box for each question.
If you answer "Yes" to any of the questions, you must attach additional information as described in the instructions.

It is our belief that you'll probably answer "No" to more than half the questions.

The questions are too lengthy and too intensive to present them verbatim here. Besides, you should read them directly off of Form

706 yourself. The questions are trying to establish what prior-to-death transfers of property interests you may have made, or may have received. The questions refer to specific tax code sections and to specific pages of the instructions for more information.

For example, the first such question (item 6) reads—

Does the gross estate contain any section 2044 property (qualified terminable interest property (QTIP) from a prior gift or estate) (see page 10 of instructions)? ☐ *Yes,* ☐*No.*

The referenced instructions read—

If you answered "Yes," these assets must be shown on Schedule F. Section 2044 property is property for which a previous section 2056(b)(7) election (QTIP election) has been made, or for which a similar gift tax election (section 2523) has been made. For more information, see the instructions on the back of Schedule F. . . . **You must complete Schedule F and file it with the return.**

This gives you an idea of why we think you should read each of the Part 4 Continuation questions yourself, and follow up on the references as needed. As to the references to sections of the IR Code, visit your local public library or your tax professional's office, and photocopy them. While at it, you may want to consult on these and other related questions.

Following the completion of Part 4: General Information, there is Part 5: *Reconciliation*. The term "reconciliation" summarizes the assets in your gross estate, and the expenses and deductions allowed against your gross estate. Schedules A through I are asset schedules, whereas Schedules J through U are deduction schedules. Obviously, you can't even begin Part 5 until all of the applicable schedules are completed. Hence, skip over Part 5 for the time being. We'll come back to it shortly below.

Schedules A through U

The "heavy duty" of Form 706 is its nine asset schedules: A through I. Together, they constitute your gross estate. Your total gross estate, in turn, constitutes Step 1 in the tax computation process in Part 2 above. There is just no way around it. To know the value of your gross estate and how it is derived, you have to fill in all of those schedules that are applicable to your situation. Recall our Chapter 2.

We are not going to repeat that which we have already presented in previous chapters. Our position is that, if you haven't heeded our earlier suggestions, you need to plow through each and every one of the nine asset schedules. The presumption is that each applies to you, unless you can establish that one or more do not apply. You won't know until you actually look at each schedule and read the IRS instructions thereto. Doing this while alive, we believe, will cause you to more fully appreciate what your executor will have to do after your demise.

As to your deduction schedules — J through U — much is common sense. Helpful in this regard is to think in terms of two classes of deductions, namely: (a) *expense* deductions, and (b) *bequest* deductions. The expense deductions are J, K, and L. The types of expenses covered by these schedules are:

1. Funeral expenses — Sched. J, part A
2. Administration expenses — Sched. J, part B
3. Litigation expenses — Sched. J, part C
4. Debts and claims — Sched. K, part A
5. Mortgages and liens — Sched. K, part B
6. Property casualty losses — Sched. L, part A
7. Property protection expenses — Sched. L, part B

You can actually fill out Schedules J, K, and L by following two principles. For those expenses that you simply cannot avoid, make reasonable estimates of them. Talk to family and friends, and to other knowledgeable persons who have gone through the Form 706 experience. The second principle is to prejudge those allowable expenditures that can reasonably be eliminated before death. Try to hold all expenses in check, as much as you reasonably can. Whatever is paid out of the gross estate — for professional fees, expenses, debts, claims, losses, etc. — reduces what is left to be taxed.

As to the bequest schedules M through U, the official titles are:

M — *Bequests, Etc., to Surviving Spouse*
O — *Charitable, Public, and Similar Gifts and Bequests*
U — *Qualified Conservation Easement Exclusion*

Any of those schedules can reduce your death tax significantly. Schedules M and O are most useful **after** you have exhausted your maximum exemption amount via ordinary bequests to your nonspousal and noncharitable heirs.

The instructions to Schedule M (about 3,600 words) are preprinted directly on Form 706 itself. In contrast, the instructions to Schedule O (about 2,700 words) are found in the instruction pamphlet which accompanies Form 706. On *each* schedule, after listing the bequests of property interests and totaling the amounts, three computational lines appear. Said lines are—

a. *Federal estate taxes payable out of property interests listed* $ \underline{\hspace{2cm}}

b. *Other death taxes payable out of property interests listed* \underline{\hspace{2cm}}

c. *Federal and state GST taxes payable out of property interests listed* \underline{\hspace{2cm}}

When added together, a, b, and c are *subtracted* from the bequeathed amounts. This subtraction reduces the net amount of dollar bequests to Schedules M and O recipients. Without this reduction, all other heirs and beneficiaries would have their property transfers diminished by the estate tax equivalent of transfers to M and O recipients.

Part 5: Recapitulation Now

Previously, we suggested that you skip over Part 5: Recapitulation, until you have completed Schedules A through I (for assets in your gross estate) and Schedules J through U (for deductions against your gross estate). Now that you have completed the schedules that apply, you have the task of entering their bottom line amounts onto Part 5. For your filling-in purposes, omit the *Alternate Value* column for Schedules A through I. As edited , we are reproducing Part 5 in Figure 12.2.

FORM 706	Part 5 - RECAPITULATION	
Item No.	**Gross Estate**	**Value at Date of Death**
1	Schedule A - Real Estate	
2	Schedule B - Stocks and Bonds	
3	Schedule C - Mortgages, Notes, and Cash	
4	Schedule D - Insurance on the Decedent's life	
5	Schedule E - Jointly Owned Property	
6	Schedule F - Other Miscellaneous Property	
7	Schedule G - Transfers During Decedent's Life	
8	Schedule H - Powers of Appointment	
9	Schedule I - Annuities	
10	Total gross estate (add items 1 through 9)	
11	Schedule U - Conservation Easement Exclusion	
12	Total Gross Estate less exclusion (subtract item 11 from item 10). Enter here and on line 1 of the tax computation.	
Item No.	**Deductions**	**Amount**
13	Schedule J - Funeral and Administration Expenses	
14	Schedule K - Debts of the Decedent	
15	Schedule K - Mortgages and Liens	
16	Total of items 13 through 15	
17	Allowable amount of deductions from item 16	
18	Schedule L - Net Losses During Administration	
19	Schedule L - Expenses Incurred in Administering Property NOT Subject to Claims	
20	Schedule M - Bequests, etc., to Surviving Spouse	
21	Schedule O - Charitable, Public, and Similar Bequests	
22	Total allowable deductions (add items 13 through 21). Enter here and on line 2 of the Tax Computation	

Fig. 12.2 - The Recapitulation of Form 706 Schedules A through O

As indicated, Part 5 is arranged into two portions, namely—

Gross Estate: Items 1 through 12

Deductions: *Items 13 through 21*

In the gross estate portion of the recapitulation instructions, there is a bold printed leadoff statement that reads:

You must make an entry in each of items 1 through 9.

This instruction is followed by an explanation as to why you "must make" an entry on each line. Said explanation reads—

*If the gross estate does not contain any assets of the type specified by a given item, **enter zero** for that item. Entering zero for any of items 1 through 9 is a statement by the executor, made under penalties of perjury, that the gross estate does not contain any includible asset covered by that item.*

Other instructions to Items 1 through 9 refer you back to specific questions that you answered in Part 4:   General Information. If you answered "Yes" to certain questions, you must attach the relevant schedule to explain why there are no assets to report on Form 706. Omissions of life insurance, annuities, and "irrevocable" trusts tend to be suspect by the IRS.

The only instruction of significance regarding deduction items 13 through 22, is item 17. Here, you get into a technical matter, called: *property subject to claims.* This is property in Schedules A through I where debts outstanding, judgment liens, tax liens, mortgage defaults, and other liability claims have not been settled at time of death. The instructions for item 17 read—

*If the amount on item 16 is more than the value of the property subject to claims, enter **the greater of** (a) the value of the property subject to claims, or (b) the amount actually paid at the time the return is filed.*

Items 12 and 22 in Part 5 (and also in Figure 12.2) read, respectively, as—

12.   *Total gross estate less exclusion (subtract item 11 from item 10). Enter here and on line 1 of Tax Computation.*

22. *Total allowable deductions (add items 17 through 22. Enter here and on line 2 of Tax Computation.*

As you may recall, the "Tax Computation" is Part 2, on page 1 of Form 706. We'll address Part 2 at the end of this chapter.

Before doing any tax computations on Form 706, you should be thinking past year 2009 . . . just in case (you live past then). Many of the Form 706 questions and schedules will continue, we believe, in a reformulated version. The most immediate revision will be the addition of: *Adjusted carryover basis* to the nine asset schedules (A through I) in Figure 12.2. As Form 706 now stands, all nine schedules are formatted with three columns in the right-hand half of each schedule. Though the columns are officially *un*lettered, we letter them as follows:

Col. A — *Alternate valuation date* _____
Col. B — *Alternate value* _____
Col. C — *Value at date of death* _____

Our recommendation at this point is that you gather together a complete blank set of the nine asset schedules, A through I. Our assumption is that you've already obtained (from the IRS's forms center or from its web site) a copy of Form 706 and its instructions. Detach (or photocopy) the nine asset schedules into a separate file or bundle of their own. Strike out the preprinted columnar captions and recaption them as follows:

Col. A — **Valuation date** _____
Col. B — **Adjusted carryover basis** $_____
Col. C — **Fair market value** $_____
        (on Col. A date)

Even if you disregard everything else in this chapter, you should take the time required and make the effort necessary to complete — in good faith — each of the Form 706 asset schedules recaptioned as above. Helpful in this regard, we believe, is Figure 12.3. Your first-hand experience in this effort will put you years ahead, decisions ahead, and documents ahead of any and all of your contemporaries.

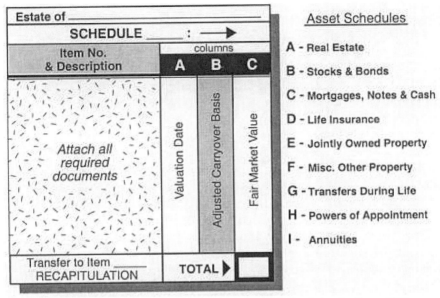

Fig. 12.3 - Columnar Recaptions on Asset Schedules to Form 706

For example, suppose that on Schedule B (706): Stocks and Bonds, you entered in the description column:

2.115 sh XYZ stock at $29.52/sh

Over a year ago, you purchased 2,000 sh of the XYZ stock for $25.00/sh. The added 115 shares were due to dividend rollovers. You'd enter in the recaptioned columns B and C as follows:

Col. C — Fair market value
    (2.115 sh x $29.52/sh) $62,435
Col. B — Adjusted carryover basis
    (2,000 sh x $25.00/sh)   <u>$50,000</u>
               Basis spread = $12,435

The basis spread is 19.92% of FMV (12,435 ÷ 62,435).

Having a basis spread of less than 20% of FMV presents a unique decision-making opportunity. Do you sell the XYZ stock while alive and you pay the capital gain tax on it, or do you bequeath the shares to your heirs and let your executor pay the estate tax on it?

For comparison, the 15% capital gains tax would be $1,865 ($12,435 x 0.15); the 35% estate tax would be $21,852 ($62,435 x 0.35). This is a $20,000 tax difference, depending on what you do or do not do while alive.

Putting It All Together

Now is the time to turn back to page 1 of Form 706 and focus on its Part 2 — *Tax Computation*. To appreciate the full 706 experience, you have to go through the computational steps yourself. We will simplify them for you. We know that all of the 20 preprinted steps will not apply in your case. The basic ones will apply, and such is the sequence we want to present. So that you'll understand the steps better, we need to make a few simplifying assumptions. After all, we are preparing *estimates* only.

Our first assumption is that all of your prior estate planning activities — wills, trusts, life estates, annuities, taxable gifts, etc. — took place **after** October 22, 1986. This was the date of enactment of the Tax Reform Act of 1986 (P.L. 99-514), which made sweeping changes in the Internal Revenue Code. The unified gift/death credit concept was instituted then.

Secondly, we are assuming that all your Schedules A through I assets are located within the U.S., and that you have inherited no property from other decedents within the past 10 years. This assumption eliminates your need for Schedule P: *Credit for Foreign Death Taxes*, and Schedule Q: *Credit for Tax on Prior Transfers*. Since these are credit schedules, any entry on them would help reduce your Form 706 tax.

With the above assumptions, the complete death tax computational sequence is presented in Figure 12.4. For each step, you can fill in your own numbers, using those developed from your own estate "as adjusted.".

Simply to help step you through Figure 12.4, we are presenting example numbers of our own. As such, we are assuming that your gross estate is $5,000,000 and that you have willed $3,000,000 in direct skips to your grandchildren. We are also assuming the year 2007, when the unified credit is $780,000 (which is equivalent to a

$2,000,000 exemption amount for that year). Furthermore, you made $250,000 in taxable gifts during life, but you paid no actual gift tax. You paid to the state of California $350,000 in inheritance tax (an illustrative assumption on our part).

FORM 706	Part 2 - TAX COMPUTATION		
Step	Description	Instruction	Amount
1	Total gross estate	From line 12 Reconciliation	$5,000,000
2	Total deductions	From line 22 Reconciliation	365,000
3	Taxable estate	Subtract step 2 from step 1	4,635,000
4	Total taxable gifts	From latest filed Form 709	250,000
5	Adjusted taxable estate	Add steps 3 and 4	4,885,000
6	TENTATIVE TAX	From Table A Instructions	2,136,750
7	Gift tax payable	From latest filed Form 709	- 0 -
8	Adjusted estate tax	Subtract step 7 from step 6	2,136,750
9	MAXIMUM UNIFIED CREDIT	For year 2007 (Figure 2.1 on p. 2-4)	780,800
10	Tentative net tax	Subtract step 9 from step 8	1,355,950
11	Credit for state death tax	Actually paid	350,000
12	Net estate tax	Subtract step 11 from step 10	1,005,950
13	GST TAX	From Sch. R, part 2, line 10	337,730
14	TOTAL TRANSFER TAX	ADD steps 12 and 13	1,343,680

Make check payable to United States Treasury
Write decedent's name, SSN, and "Form 706"

Fig. 12.4 - Basic Steps for Estimating Your Death Tax With Form 706

For skip persons (your grandchildren and great grandchildren), before the GST tax applies, the same estate tax exemption is allowed. Thus, for our assumptions above, using Schedule R of Form 706, the GST tax becomes $337,730 (approximately).

Completion and Conclusion

For the numbers that we have entered in Figure 12.4, your total transfer tax turns out to be: $1,343,680. Thus, of your $5,000,000 gross estate, your heirs (nonskips and skip persons) will receive $3,291,320 [5,000,000 – 365,000 expenses – 1,343,680 tax]. Of this amount, you have earmarked 35% for your two children (nonskip persons) and 65% for your four grandchildren (or skip persons). In the meantime, all six of these heirs each received separately $12,000 each year which qualified for your annual gift tax exclusions.

With this information, you can now finally complete the *Amount* column for items 4 and 5 in Part 4: ***General Information***. The item 4 amount would be whatever you entered on Schedule M: Bequests to Surviving Spouse. If your spouse had a $5,000,000 gross estate of her own, your Schedule M would likely be zero. Thus, the item 5 amounts might be:

Child A	575,981}	
Child B	575,981}	$1,151,962
Grandchild 1	534,840}	
Grandchild 2	534,840}	
Great-grandchild x	534,839}	$2,139,358
Great-grandchild y	534,839}	
	3,291,320	

With this item 5 entry in Part 4, your draft Form 706 should be as complete as you can possibly make it . . . while you're alive.

What is the conclusion that we want you to come to?

We want you to conclude that computing — estimating, really — your death tax while alive is an entirely different experience from that derived from your annual Forms 1040 that you have, or will have, filed over 35 to 50 years throughout life. Form 706 is so different that only the **rare person** — such as yourself — actually undergoes the experience. Therefore, our contention is that by experiencing Form 706 now, you'll develop much better insight into why the organization of your estate is so necessary.

ABOUT
THE AUTHOR

Holmes F. Crouch

Born on a small farm in southern Maryland, Holmes was graduated from the U.S. Coast Guard Academy with a Bachelor's Degree in Marine Engineering. While serving on active duty, he wrote many technical articles on maritime matters. After attaining the rank of Lieutenant Commander, he resigned to pursue a career as a nuclear engineer.

Continuing his education, he earned a Master's Degree in Nuclear Engineering from the University of California. He also authored two books on nuclear propulsion. As a result of the tax write-offs associated with writing these books, the IRS audited his returns. The IRS's handling of the audit procedure so annoyed Holmes that he undertook to become as knowledgeable as possible regarding tax procedures. He became a licensed private Tax Practitioner by passing an examination administered by the IRS. Having attained this credential, he started his own tax preparation and counseling business in 1972.

In the early years of his tax practice, he was a regular talk-show guest on San Francisco's KGO Radio responding to hundreds of phone-in tax questions from listeners. He was a much sought-after guest speaker at many business seminars and taxpayer meetings. He also provided counseling on special tax problems, such as divorce matters, property exchanges, timber harvesting, mining ventures, animal breeding, independent contractors, selling businesses, and offices-at-home. Over the past 25 years, he has prepared nearly 10,000 tax returns for individuals, estates, trusts, and small businesses (in partnership and corporate form).

During the tax season of January through April, he prepares returns in a unique manner. During a single meeting, he completes the return . . . *on the spot!* The client leaves with his return signed, sealed, and in a stamped envelope. His unique approach to preparing returns and his personal interest in his clients' tax affairs have honed his professional proficiency. His expertise extends through itemized deductions, computer-matching of income sources, capital gains and losses, business expenses and cost of goods, residential rental expenses, limited and general partnership activities, closely-held corporations, to family farms and ranches.

He remembers spending 12 straight hours completing a doctor's complex return. The next year, the doctor, having moved away, utilized a large accounting firm to prepare his return. Their accountant was so impressed by the manner in which the prior return was prepared that he recommended the doctor travel the 500 miles each year to have Holmes continue doing it.

He recalls preparing a return for an unemployed welder, for which he charged no fee. Two years later the welder came back and had his return prepared. He paid the regular fee . . . and then added a $300 tip.

During the off season, he represents clients at IRS audits and appeals. In one case a shoe salesman's audit was scheduled to last three hours. However, after examining Holmes' documentation it was concluded in 15 minutes with "no change" to his return. In another instance he went to an audit of a custom jeweler that the IRS dragged out for more than six hours. But, supported by Holmes' documentation, the client's return was accepted by the IRS with "no change."

Then there was the audit of a language translator that lasted two full days. The auditor scrutinized more than $1.25 million in gross receipts, all direct costs, and operating expenses. Even though all expensed items were documented and verified, the auditor decided that more than $23,000 of expenses ought to be listed as capital items for depreciation instead. If this had been enforced it would have resulted in a significant additional amount of tax. Holmes strongly disagreed and after many hours of explanation got the amount reduced by more than 60% on behalf of his client.

He has dealt extensively with gift, death and trust tax returns. These preparations have involved him in the tax aspects of wills, estate planning, trustee duties, probate, marital and charitable bequests, gift and death exemptions, and property titling.

Although not an attorney, he prepares Petitions to the U.S. Tax Court for clients. He details the IRS errors and taxpayer facts by citing pertinent sections of tax law and regulations. In a recent case involving an attorney's ex-spouse, the IRS asserted a tax deficiency of $155,000. On behalf of his client, he petitioned the Tax Court and within six months the IRS conceded the case.

Over the years, Holmes has observed that the IRS is not the industrious, impartial, and competent federal agency that its official public imaging would have us believe.

He found that, at times, under the slightest pretext, the IRS has interpreted against a taxpayer in order to assess maximum penalties, and may even delay pending matters so as to increase interest due on additional taxes. He has confronted the IRS in his own behalf on five separate occasions, going before the U.S. Claims Court, U.S. District Court, and U.S. Tax Court. These were court actions that tested specific sections of the Internal Revenue Code which he found ambiguous, inequitable, and abusively interpreted by the IRS.

Disturbed by the conduct of the IRS and by the general lack of tax knowledge by most individuals, he began an innovative series of taxpayer-oriented Federal tax guides. To fulfill this need, he undertook the writing of a series of guidebooks that provide in-depth knowledge on one tax subject at a time. He focuses on subjects that plague taxpayers all throughout the year. Hence, his formulation of the "Allyear" Tax Guide series.

The author is indebted to his wife, Irma Jean, and daughter, Barbara MacRae, for the word processing and computer graphics that turn his experiences into the reality of these publications. Holmes welcomes comments, questions, and suggestions from his readers. He can be contacted in California at (408) 867-2628, or by writing to the publisher's address.

ALLYEAR Tax Guides
by Holmes F. Crouch

Series 100 - INDIVIDUALS AND FAMILIES

Series 200 - INVESTORS AND BUSINESSES

Series 300 - RETIREES AND ESTATES

Series 400 - OWNERS AND SELLERS

Series 500 - AUDITS AND APPEALS

For information about the above titles, contact
Holmes F. Crouch

Allyear Tax Guides

Phone: (408) 867-2628   Fax: (408) 867-6466